Presented to:

_____

From:

_____

Date:

_____

MAN...
Again

The Way To Love and To Be Loved

By

Alfredo Mendoza

Orange, CA

A MAN...

...Is not the man who looks the most like a man

>Nor is a man the man that shouts the loudest and scares

>Nor is more man the man with the most tattoos and metals on his face

>>A man is the man that carries integrity in his words.

...A man is not the man who has the most women so he can impress

>Nor is a man the man that endures the most drugs or drinks

>>A man is the man that has only one woman

>>And one thirst to satisfy her

Introduction

Let me ask you a question before we start sharing resources (you: time and me: information). I don't want you to waste your time doing something that is not of your interest, nor do I want to talk to someone unable to value this information. Here is the question:

If everything you have heard about how to be a Man turns out to be false, by when would you like to know the truth, today or tomorrow? If your response to this question is: "**right away!!**", then this information is for you. Your time will be well invested here.

WARNING: This information will challenge the way you think about the Male-Female relationship conduct. It will defy the socially accepted ideas of how to be masculine or feminine, the leader of the relationship, the Man that knows how to love and is loved in return.

This book is intended to be experienced not just read. This experience will be similar to you and I walking into a dark mine filled up with nuggets of common sense and wisdom. Don't be scared. I walked into the dark mine myself already. I came out of it alive. I came out of it a wiser man.

The advice I received from other people (personal experiences, real life stories, coaches, writers, studies, surveys, etc.) who visited the mine before me, guided me to examine the darkest areas on my path and find effective solutions to create happier relationships. See: the exam is much easier if someone gives you the answers to questions prior to you taking the test. Most likely, you will get an A+ on it, wouldn't you? It is always better to have the answers with you in advance. This way, you can assure healthy relationships. I will share common solutions for you to solve relationship problems and enjoy them more.

So, leave your bag of disbelieve hanging outside the entrance door. Open your heart and your mind as if they were empty bags ready to receive the goodies to fill them up. You are about to collect nuggets of wisdom pertaining the creation of effective and loving relationships between a man and a woman. These nuggets of wisdom will be yours to keep at the end of our journey.

It is your responsibility, as a MAN to a woman and, as the leader of the pack, to better the life of your future generations by sharing and transferring your love and wisdom to your descendants. The body of a Man disappears from this world once he dies, but not the wisdom he implanted to his descendants. A MAN that loves and receives love in return is a HAPPY MAN. It is the MAN's responsibility to create his own happiness.

Respectfully,

Alfredo Mendoza

My Realization

I was having lunch with two of my female friends, Maggie and Michelle. Michelle has been married and divorced twice. Her marriages did not last for more than 7 years, each. Maggie has been married for almost 50 years and still going strong in her marriage.

We talked about the ups and downs of men and women in relationships. Why some relationships last for so long versus others don't even take off the ground. I listened to their conversation and opinions very carefully. I was sucking their personal stories and the experiences they lived with their partners while living together. They also chatted about the reasons why their relationships broke down. They allowed me to enter into their mine of experiences. I listened to their nuggets of wisdom.

I was deep in thought when, Suddenly, I hear: "What about you, Alfredo? What caused your two marriages to fail?" This question hit me deeply and snapped me out of limbo, like a woman slapping a man on his cheek. I answered the question within five seconds.

"I didn't know how to be a man," I said. "Yes, I did not know how to be the Man in the relationship," I repeated thoughtfully, looking into the distance, nodding my head up and down, side to side, slowly. "I didn't know how to be a Man."

Maggie replied promptly, "What do you mean you did not know how to be a man? You are a man, first of all. You are a hardworking man. I saw you providing for your family. Your wife drove a nice car. She was pretty. She did not work. She was well dressed each time I saw her. I don't remember complaining about her not being well taken care of when we spoke with each other. I am willing to say they had everything they needed with you. Your children always looked presentable and were respectful. So, how can you say you did not know how to be a man?"

"I don't buy it! I think you are pulling our leg, Alfredo," Michelle complained. "Did you cheat on your wives?" She curiously inquired.

"No! I was loyal to her, very loyal! I answered. "From work to my house and back again, 5 days a week, 12 hours a day; 3 hours sitting on the freeway, daily. No time to cheat!" I responded.

"Then, why would you say you did not know how to be a man? Explain….," Maggie demanded.

"I allowed for my women to be the man of the relationship," I said. "I was weak as a man. At the time, when I was in the relationship, I thought I was behaving as a man. I followed the patterns of our society's expectation on how a man ought to act. I applied a little bit of experience and advice my father transferred over to me. Neither one worked. So, here I am: Solo," I told them.

"Wait a minute, Alfredo. How can you not know how to be a man? I still do not understand?" Maggie asked me.

"Maggie," I replied, "I have studied men-women relationships, asked divorced people, married couples, read books, asked authorities on psychology and human behavior, watched videos, reviewed surveys and studies from private and public entities about healthy relationships. I have discovered that I was not behaving as the man of my house. I was just a guy occupying space in a house, roommate to a woman, and paying for the family bills, and did not even realize it."

I continued, "It is humbling and, at the same time, I feel liberated to understand and accept the down faults I provided to my partners as a man. I completed an auto-analysis on my past approaches and actions as a man within my relationships and discover this: Almost everything I have observed socially and have been thought by my parents all my life about been a man, *was dead wrong*. I did almost everything wrong. I have become so good at analyzing relationships that I can watch couples walking on the street and more or less know the status of the relationship. I can see a man and a woman interact with each other and have an almost accurate guess who is the masculine and who is the feminine. I can tell you, without guilt, I did not know how to guide my relationships. I paid the price for it. However, now I know what makes a man... A MAN".

Maggie and Michelle kept quiet, as if they were confused, yet interested about my discovery. They asked me to tell them more about my discovery on how to be A MAN. "I am!" I told them. I will tell you all about it in the book I am going to write. They encouraged me to write it. We finished our food, walked out of the restaurant, and parted our own ways. You have the book in your hands now!

Special Dedication

To

Heavenly Father for granting me patience and wisdom to persevere in the completion of this meaningful and pleasurable journey. Every step of the way, you were there with me; lonely hours, days, months, and years, but you were there with me. I felt you.

I dedicate this book to *myself*, primarily, for accepting the challenge to explore my life on this earth as a human being and, more importantly, as a Man, for fostering the courage, the patience, the discipline, and the deep desire to discover and reinvent myself. For being interested in exploring my failures, my parents teachings, social dogmas, my weaknesses and strengths, my past, present and future life. For walking into a path I knew it would be emotionally and mentally defiant. For having an open heart and mind to accept the teachings of other people that, just like me, made the decision to become better human beings, a better woman and man.

These teachings are dedicated to my son, Freddy. He has the potential to become a man of integrity, a person of substance and meaningful to him and others, a man with high standards, so when he gets caught-up with the fashions and immediate-gratification of temptations, pleasures and the daily life challenges, he has the character, and the guts, to stay above negative influences and make beneficial decisions. I wish for him to become a man of honor, a man of his word, an extraordinary man, willing to stand up for great values and principals beneficial to him, his family, his home, and his business, a value-contributing citizen of our society. I wish for him to be a worthy example for his sisters, children, and friends; an example worth emulating, the husband, the man, and the leader that provides trust and confidence to his woman, the man of his home, the leader of his pack and his destiny. I wish for him to become a coveted trophy.

To my daughters: Paloma, Citlali, Xochilt, Perla, and Kassandra. I invested the most valuable resource I have: time. I want to share with you, as a Man and as a father, the factors you need to consider when dating men among men. Hopefully, from this crowd of men, your Man, your husband, the father of your children will show up. Don't settle for looks or nationalities. Nor do you tolerate abuse from any one, let alone Men. Don't be afraid to let go of incompatible men. Don't be scare to be alone. Be afraid to be with someone that takes you for granted! I wish for you to find your ideal man. Foster the strength to select the man that will value, respect, and appreciate you for who you are and will become. The man willing and able to participate and promote your personal evolution as a woman, spouse, and as a mother. You become a person of value and substance, a partner that proudly walks on the right side next to her husband, the phenomenal mother your children deserve to have.

Don't get caught-up with social dogmas and new fashions about men and women in our society. You do what is right for you and your family. You make your own decisions on your own thinking and in your life. Value yourself and your partner. Never compare yourself to a Man. We are different. Heavenly Father made us different. Men and women are a complement to each other. A home is not a home if either of the parents is missing. Transform your Man's house into a home. Give your children a chance to have a loving home and a perpetual family. Don't be afraid to be feminine and share it with your partner. Be a coveted trophy.

To my parents: My foundation. The have been the two columns of strength to my only sister and 7 brothers. They tattooed a great example of perseverance within us. They made great efforts to show us a loving and respectful family life. They transferred over to me their experiences, ideas, and opinions to the best of their ability. All their sermons have taught me something about relationships and life itself. I am thankful to my father, the hunter, the protector, the die-hard, for bringing the bacon home. I am grateful to my mother for cooking the bacon, so I would not go hungry. She, freely and unselfishly, shared with me her motherly love and care. Oh, it is beautiful to have a caring woman like her, proudly feminine, as my mother. My father showed me that, regardless the age, it is beautiful to hug and kiss your own children. I wish he would have kissed my mother more, though. He did as he knew. My mother showed me to feed the less fortunate, specially, if they are close to your own family. We were not rich, but I would not change my parents nor my childhood for anything in the world.

Lastly, to men and women in the world, who have a hard time, and fight daily, understanding the opposite gender. They are willing to reinvent themselves to become better men or women, better family leaders at home, at their community and in business. Especially, to divorcees, singles, married couples with a broken heart and fading hopes. There is a way out, as long as you are willing to re-invent and re-engineer yourself. So, be willing to open your heart and mind to a new way of handling relationships, a new way of life as new MAN.

~Alfredo Mendoza~

Table of Contents

1	|	Relationships 101	| page 1
2	|	What Men and Women Want?	| Page 19
3	|	A Ride to Memory Lane	| Page 31
4	|	Male Feminization And Female Masculinization	| Page 37
5	|	Women Appreciation Movement	| Page 49
6	|	Men and Dogs	| Page 55
7	|	Women and Cats	| Page 61
8	|	Secret Energies	| Page 67
9	|	The Eva Case	| Page 103
10	|	Relationships: ALPHA, BETA, GAMA	| Page 123
11	|	The Best Couple: Lazy and Polarity	| Page 129
12	|	The Moment of Truth	| Page 141
13	|	You Are the Trophy	| Page 149
14	|	Life of a Relationship	| Page 161
15	|	Signs of Attraction	| Page 177

16	|	Temporary Vs. Permanent Relationships	|Page 205
17	|	Prenuptial Agreement	|Page 243
18	|	Drama-Free Circle	|Page 251
19	|	Keep the Flame Burning and Going	|Page 255
20	|	A Mirror Has Two Faces	|Page 291
21	|	Share and Transfer the secrets	|Page 301
	|	About the Author	|Page 307
	|	About REVIVE Institute	|Page 309

RELATIONSHIPS

1 0 1

A relationship is an investment. It requires you to invest the most precious resources you possess: time, energy and money. You can always recharge energy and make more money. Time, you would agree, once it has been used up, it does not come back. So if you are going to invest your resources in a relationship, doesn't it make sense for you to REALLY know what you are investing your resources in? I lived 13 years with one person and 7 years with another person neither of whom wanted the same things I wanted in a relationship, in a family, and in life. We all were good people, just not good for each other. Not a good investment! I should have scrutinized my investment thoroughly. I was thinking with a different head.

So, what is the right investment? Well, there are three types of relationship investments to consider. You MUST be able to understand them with clarity, so when these investments show up, you can determine if they are worth your time to go after and acquire them. Here we go:

Type 1: Exterior beauty Investment

Type 2: Interior beauty Investment

Type 3: Type 1 and 2 investment combination.

Fortunately for you, you are the only one who can make the last decision on the type of investment you would like to consider and eventually own. Only you know what turns you on. Only you know your reasons. Each relationship investment will pay you dividends; some good, others not so good. Your only job is to decide the type of dividends (consequences) you are willing to accept. Some investment dividends will bring you happiness, while others will lead to misery.

And so, again, before you start investing your time, money and energy, you must understand your investment choices, know the type of dividends, before jumping into "the pool," the person you want to be with, most likely will return to you. You are totally responsible for your investment, because you will be the sole recipient of the consequences. So, invest wisely.

The story below circulated on several websites throughout the internet. This story does a great job of explaining perfectly a type 1 investment: External Beauty. We are lucky, the story comes with a bonus attached to it: THE ANSWER.

Type 1 Investment: External Beauty:

What Am I Doing Wrong?

Okay, I'm tired of beating around the bush. I'm a beautiful (spectacularly beautiful) 25 year old girl. I'm articulate and classy. I'm not from New York. I'm looking to get married to a guy who makes at least half a million a year. I know how that sounds, but keep in mind that a million a year is middle class in New York City, so I don't think I'm overreaching at all.

Are there any guys who make 500K or more on this board? Any wives? Could you send me some tips? I dated a business man who makes average around 200k - 250k. But that's where I seem to hit a roadblock. 250,000 won't get me to central park west. I know a woman in my Yoga class who was married to an investment banker and lives in Tribeca, and she's not as pretty as I am, nor is she a great genius. So what is she doing right? How do I get to her level?

Here are my questions specifically:

- Where do you single rich men hang out? Give me specifics — bars, restaurants, gyms...

- What are you looking for in a mate? Be honest guys, you won't hurt my feelings...

- Is there an age range I should be targeting (I'm 25)?

- Why are some of the women living lavish lifestyles on the Upper East Side so plain? I've seen really 'plain Jane' boring types who have nothing to offer married to incredibly wealthy guys. I've seen drop dead gorgeous girls in singles bars in the east village. What's the story there?

- Jobs I should look out for? Everyone knows - lawyer, investment banker, doctor. How much do those guys really make? And where do they hang out? Where do the hedge fund guys hang out?

- How you decide marriage vs. just a girlfriend? I am looking for MARRIAGE ONLY

Please hold your insults — I'm putting myself out there in an honest way. Most beautiful women are superficial; at least I'm being up front about it. I wouldn't be searching for these kind of guys if I wasn't able to match them — in looks, culture, sophistication, and keeping a nice home and hearth.

It's NOT ok to contact this poster with services or other commercial interests

THE ANSWER

Dear Pers-431649184:

I read your posting with great interest and have thought meaningfully about your dilemma. I offer the following analysis of your predicament. I also have a great proposition for you:

Firstly, I'm not wasting your time, I qualify as a guy who fits your bill; that is I make more than $500K per year. That said here's how I see it.

Your offer, from the prospective of a guy like me, is a plain and simple business deal. Here's why. Cutting through all the B.S., what you suggest is a simple trade: you bring your looks to the party and I bring my money. Fine, simple. But here's the rub, your looks will fade with time and my money will likely continue to grow into perpetuity... in fact, it is very likely that my income increases but it is an absolute certainty that you won't be getting any more beautiful!

So, in economic terms, you are a depreciating asset and I am an earning asset. Not only are you a depreciating asset, your depreciation accelerates! Let me explain, you're 25 now and will likely stay pretty hot for the next 5 years, but less so each year. We call this: diminishing returns. Then the fade begins in earnest. By 35 stick a fork in you!

So in Wall Street terms, we would call you a trading position, not a buy and hold... hence the rub... marriage. It doesn't make good business sense to "buy you" (which is what you're asking) so I'd rather lease you. In case you think I'm being cruel, I would say the following. If my money were to go away, so would you. So when your beauty fades, I need an out. It's as simple as that. So, a deal that makes sense for me is dating, friends with benefits, not marriage.

Separately, I was taught early at school about efficient markets. So, I wonder, why a girl as "articulate, classy and spectacularly beautiful" as you, has been unable to find a sugar-daddy? I find it hard to believe that if you are as gorgeous as you say you are that the $500K hasn't found you, at least for a tryout.

By the way, you could always find a way to make your own money and then we wouldn't need to have this difficult conversation.

With all that said, I must say you're going about it the right way for the classic "pump and dump."

So, I propose leasing you. It is a good deal for both of us. You enjoy my money while you are with me and I enjoy your beauty while it lasts; fair game. As you can see, I am taking your words on a face value that you are "spectacularly beautiful". Do send me your full-body picture so I can see your investment offering. Once we agree on each other's offering, we can sign a lease agreement right away. A renewable yearly lease agreement is best. This way, if I run out of money, you can walk away freely and, if I get tired of you, I can drop you at the end of the contract. Let me know. -Post: 046542-

Boy! Am I familiar with this concept!

Are you in for a "Pump-and-Dump" investment? Basically, she pumps as much money as possible out of you and then dumps you once she drains you dry. The choice is yours. You decide if this external investment if good for you. You will be the recipient of your investment returns, anyhow. You made your own decision. So, do not blame others for the consequences. It is on you and only YOU.

How do you detect a person that wants to attract another person based on external beauty? She uses her beauty ONLY to gain material benefits and does not care about engaging emotionally or sentimentally with another person. She places low interest on strong values and principals. She expects for you to have money so you can earn her attention. She never pays or volunteers to pay anything. She hates other pretty and desirable women. She wants the gold and the castle but is not willing to work for it. She wants short-term relationships. She expects a special treatment everywhere she goes just because she is pretty. She is constantly looking around to see who is watching her when in public. The most important factor I can give you to promptly uncover this type of person is this: these people are not always willing to engage and honestly show and give any type of sincere or emotional affection to another person. The focus is on them, ONLY.

Type 2 Investment: Interior beauty

This type of interior investment deals purely with values and principals. You are investing on the essence, the core, of the person with whom you want to form a relationship: sentiments and emotions. You are investing in a good person. She might not be the most beautiful woman on the block, but she has great feelings and a great sense of humor. This type of investment becomes very profound and more meaningful with time. She genuinely cares. It is like a good wine, the older it gets, and the better it is. These are the investments worth keeping. These investments are worthwhile searching for! Like I said before, the only one able to determine if this relationship is for you is YOU. The movie Forest Gump illustrates this type of relationship:

Forrest Gump was born with a mental and physical disability, if you remember. He cannot talk very well. He has a hard time processing thoughts quickly. He can barely walk. He has, however, a good heart. His "friends" made fun of and mistreated him. He did not hold a grudge against them. He still treated people with respect. He minded his own business. He meets Jennie and falls in love with her. Love at first sight. From the moment Forrest heard the voice of that little girl on the school bus, his world changed. He became devoted to Jennie.

He invested a lot of time hanging around Jennie: playing, talking about the future, sharing emotions and sentiments, holding hands, hugging as children, etc. They grew up and split apart. Jennie leaves Forrest behind and goes out to experience life. She forgets about Forrest while Forrest's loyalty to her continued. His feelings and emotions for Jennie grew as he aged. The more mature, the clearer Forrest's sentiments and emotions became.

Jennie becomes a drug addict, bounces from bed to bed, and becomes life careless. Forrest loved her in spite of that. He proposes marriage to her; she declines. Forrest then says to her that he might not be smart but "I know what love is" and walks away broken hearted. Jennie leaves and then returns to Forrest's house to peacefully pass away. Forrest accepts her, cares for her, and then buries her in a special place close to him.

Forrest displayed a character to love just Jennie. He understood her. He gave her patience and understanding. When she was ill lying in bed, he took care of her. He expressed his inner sentiments and emotions to her by his actions while not compromising his values and principals.

Forrest himself is a great example of interior beauty. Unfortunately, Forrest Gump picked the wrong investment with Jennie. Jennie did not perceive interior beauty as a valuable investment. Their relationship and expectations were not in sync. These are the results when a person becomes a devotee to the wrong person.

How do you recognize internal beauty? She treats others with kindness and is a fair person. She is fun to have around. She is playful, can take and make a joke. She expresses a high level of appreciation for everything she owns. She loves to help with causes she believes in. She respects her parents and people over all, most importantly, always takes care of her siblings and parents. She is spiritually faithful. Expressing her emotions and feelings comes natural to her. She wants to discover you, but not your money, you, the real you. She asks questions about your present and your future. She is centered and wants to confirm that your values and principals are similar, or almost similar to hers. They are conversational. They express their opinions very tactfully. Many of them are constantly looking for ways to improve themselves, their relationships, their life over all. They take the time to understand what they do not comprehend. Meaningful accomplishments bring them happiness in life. *Integrity* is the <u>Numero Uno</u> priority to them. She is a loving person.

Type 3 Investment: The Ultimate Investment

This relationship is a combination of type 1 and 2 investment: The ultimate relationship. Some men call it: "the perfect relationship." This is the relationship every man in the world dreams to accomplish. *A beautiful face and body coupled with strong values and principals.* This ideal relationship is for everybody, but not everybody can have one. Only people who are centered reach this ultimate experience. It demands total maturity on the investment, the person itself. In other words, she needs to be comfortable with being pretty and desirable and able to control others and herself. The dividends this investment will return are beyond comprehension. My friend, Maggie, told me that she has cried, many times, out of happiness because she has a Good-Looking guy who values his creator, his wife, his family, his business and acts accordingly. "He is the whole enchilada", she told me. It is, however, the toughest relationship to create and consummate. It is reserved for special people willing to earn their place to hang around with the great ones. The story of Joe and Bella is a great example of this perfect relationship. I will share it with you just as Joe passed it on to me:

I met Joe and Bella almost 10 years ago at a social gathering. Bella is about 30 years old. Joe is 40 years old. They have been married for about 10 years. They have 2 children. Joe is 9 years old and Cindy, 8 years old. Joe and Bella are two, playful, grown-up "children." If I did not know them, I would have guessed that they both are still dating and trying to form a relationship. They still behave like a boyfriend and girlfriend in courtship: Holding hands, kissing publicly, hugging each other as they walk, joke around with each other, go to the movies and dancing places, etc. They were made for each other.

Bella's parents hired Joe's company to do the landscaping at their home. Joe was one of the landscape workers. Bella's family is a Caucasian, upper middle class family. Joe belonged to a low-class, Mexican family. Naturally, Joe met Bella at her home. Joe was 30 and she was 20 at the time they met each other. Joe's life changed forever on a really hot, Friday afternoon.

He was mowing the lawn and trimming bushes at Bella's home. The sun's rays and heat were almost unbearable. Something within Joe advised him to just drop the tools and quit his work. Joe refused to abandon the job; his word was much too valuable to him to just walk away from his commitment. So, he kept on working.

Suddenly, the house's main entrance door opens and a feminine, well-sculptured silhouette makes its way toward Joe and his coworker. She handed out a cold glass of water to Joe's coworker and, then, walked towards Joe's location to give him water as well. She made fresh lemonade for them. Joe heard Bella's angelic voice "I made fresh lemonade for you guys" and he accepted the lemonade. He stood still in disbelief. In front of him was the most beautiful woman he had ever seen. A perfect face, enchanting eyes, friendly smile, beautiful body, a caring woman.

He was nervous. He could not put his words together fast enough to say: "thank you." She said: "you're welcome" and her charming smile landed in Joe's heart. She told him that if they felt more thirsty to let her know. She would be happy to make more lemonade for them.

She turned and made her way back into the house. Joe stood mesmerized as he saw the silhouette of a mermaid disappearing into the house. Only her perfume, fresh like the flowers in the yard, refused to abandon him. That aroma found space inside Joe's nostrils and lungs. He inhaled it slowly, as if he was inflating his chest with her perfume. It was a life changing experience for him.

Confused with the situation, Joe, could not believe that a woman like Bella would even take the time to talk to a couple of Mexican landscapers, let alone prepare and give them fresh lemonade. He was confused, very confused.

Joe and Bella became friends. They went out, as friends, to play mini-golf, movies, restaurants, parks, to the beach, etc. He remembers those odd moments at public places being with a breath-taking, straight-out gorgeous, in your face, great looking woman. She was too desirable to almost every man in sight. Her presence, by itself, commanded attention. She just had a very feminine presence; even other women could not keep their eyes, and their boyfriend's eyes off of Bella.

At restaurants, almost everybody wanted to treat her as if she was a celebrity. Bella did not like that. She told a waiter once to treat her just as he treats everybody else. The men inside the restaurants could not get enough of her.

At one occasion, a Casanova approached Bella while Joe went to the restroom. Joe walked out of the restroom to find the Casanova standing in front of his table, next to Bella. Joe walked to the table and before he had a chance to say a word, Bella stood up, look at the Casanova and told him that she would like to introduce HER Boyfriend, Joe, to him. Joe remained gesture less, as if he was in deep thought, confused, looking at the Casanova, and smiled. The three of them remained in silence for about five seconds, which felt like an eternity, according to Joe. The Casanova walked away. Bella and Joe smiled at each other. Bella told Joe that the tough-guy "needed to learn some respect for people." She understood values and principals.

"I noticed she knew how to say thank you, you're welcome, please, it's okay, etc. She had manners," Joe commented me.

One time she even sent a note to the cooks in the kitchen to thank them for preparing such a great meal; she was conscientious and appreciative.

At another time, they saw a homeless person standing outside a Mexican restaurant, Joe gave the person 2 dollars, and Bella added another 5 dollars and told the person that 7 dollars would buy him a big burrito and a large soda. She was thoughtful and humane.

Joe and Bella dated more seriously and tied the knot 2 years after knowing each other. Joe asked Bella to tell him why she picked him for a husband. Joe knew Bella's face and body would get her just about anything or anyone she wanted! She knew rich friends she met at her private university and at family functions. There were guys that were way better looking, model like, compared to him. She responded that she was not looking for money, models, or a particular race. She was looking for a person with values and principles that closely match hers, capable of treating her as a human being. She knew herself. She understood her expectations. She was mature and centered.

Joe and Bella have two children now and they own a large landscaping company and employ over 120 employees. They can buy a BIG house. However, they prefer to live in a modest home. Although they give each other lots of freedom, they understand they have values and principles that they cherish and will not compromise. This is what every man wants in life, whether they want to accept it or not.

How do you know when a woman fits the category of the Ultimate Investment? Values and principals determine her character. She has manners, is respectful and very considerate. She is comfortable with and has under control the fact that she is beautiful, attractive, and desirable. She is a well-balanced, mature person.

2

WHAT MEN AND WOMEN WANT?

HE WANTS:

To conquer a woman. He wants to penetrate a woman psychologically, emotionally, and physically. His main objective is sexual gratification. Once a man sees a desirable, attractive woman, he wants to penetrate her. He wants to know her rapidly so he can satisfy his inner desire. If a man had a choice between investing long periods of time romancing a woman to seduce her or to have sex right away without romancing and seduction, he would almost always pick the _sex right away_ choice. Men see, like, want to touch, feel, and want to satisfy their inner urge. Men want to get the boogie on promptly by investing the least amount of resources (money, energy, time, etc...) possible.

He wants a woman of integrity. A person willing to adhere to moral and ethical principles. Someone of sound moral character, honest, with solid principles and values. For example, she helps his children with homework because she knows it is the right thing to do. She is loyal to her husband because it is morally correct. She converts her house into a home because she accepts that without her, the home is not complete. She executes the responsibility she promised her husband because she values her promises.

He wants a knowledgeable woman. It is true that men are driven by sex. However, when it comes to matters of building a relationship or family, mature men wish to engage with intelligent, mature women. He wants his woman to be able to function on her own as much as necessary. He understands a woman will need, at one time or another, when he is not able to be with her, to make her own decisions. He expects for his woman, every now and then, to be decisive and act for the benefit of the relationship or family. Men understand personal injuries and catastrophes occur in life unexpectedly. He expects for his woman to navigate those tough times with dignity and grace in his absence. He wants his woman to be intelligent with his children's upbringing and always look out for their best interest.

He wants strength in a woman. A woman capable of offering a solid upbringing to his children; one who's capable of protecting and nourishing his babies in his absence. If he is at work, he is at peace because he knows his children are safe with the woman he trusts. If he dies, he dies worry-free because he acknowledges his woman is sufficiently strong enough to manifest the goals he has laid out for his family. He wants his woman to guide his children straight on a prosperous and safe path. He expects her to teach them how to be loving, caring, and display tenderness, teaching the girls to behave as girls and boys as boys.

He wants <u>freedom</u> to focus on his purpose. He expects from his woman to understand this meaningful and essential fact. Once a man has satisfied his sexual desire, he wants to be left alone. He wants to refocus on continuing with his purpose in life, his plans, if you will. Every man has a purpose. Some men want to recreate the world, build a company, play in the NFL, become a celebrity, etc. Other men want to be plain lazy and their purpose is to have no purpose at all! But, every man has a purpose. It just depends on what type of purpose he wants to achieve in his life.

He wants an active woman who is energetic and takes care of her body, nurtures her intellect, spiritual. Men believe that if she takes care of herself, most likely she will take care of her family and home. She will create a healthy family environment.

He craves a woman with the desire to better her life and the life of her family, able to cheer up her man while he is in the trenches of life trying to build a future for her and their children. He craves a woman, wise enough to comprehend the struggles and obstacles at hand and willing to stand next to her man as a sign of her support for his goals, because she understands that two people committed to the same purpose will reach their objective.

He adores a woman unafraid to state that she is a woman, talks and acts like a woman, proud to be feminine and behaves feminine. He understands that it is important his children have an example of a feminine matured woman at home.

He needs a woman able to solve problems and not creates problems. She needs to be reasonable. A woman that does not feel superior to anyone yet, understands who she is and what she represents, a woman with a strong sense of self-worth.

SHE WANTS:

Romance and seduction. They, purposely, extend the romance and seduction times to maximize their sexual gratification. They also want sex; but not right away. They want to invest time and energy to live and create their own romantic novel. Their focus is to make a fantasy a reality. A fantasy she becomes aware of at an early age, as a little girl: Be the "Pretty Princess" and find your "Prince Charming."

She is expecting a charming Prince. A mysterious man that, suddenly, would show up in her life, out of nowhere, to romance and conquer her. The courageous person with an imposing male presence that makes her feel excited and is irresistible. An animal energy too strong for her energy to ignore. She wants a leader, a protector for her and her children, a solid rock she can lean on, a man she can respect and admire, a Prince who can be playful with her and treat her as a bratty-little sister. A man very confident with his masculinity.

She wants to experience surprise, mystery, and discovery. Women are fascinated by this three factors. A woman enjoys being surprised by her man with thoughtful details, especially if the surprise is meaningful to her. That is exciting to them. They like for their Prince Charmin to take them out, but they prefer the place or activity to remain a secret. They want to experience the discovery. Tell her you are taking her out; just don't tell her where.

Every time a man denies information to her, she develops a love-hate emotion toward him. Love because she likes the pleasure she experiences while discovering the unknown. Hate because he hides information from her. She likes mystery games. She likes for her man to walk with her the path of the unknown. She wants to experience the emotional rushes and the butterflies in her stomach as she discovers the promise land with her Prince Charming. This is a way to penetrate psychologically and emotionally a woman.

From day one, when she discovers her Prince Charming, she expects for him to make eye-contact and approach her. She wants the man to initiate courtship. She expects for the man to KNOW how to court a woman. Basically, she wants her date to take her on dates to wine and dine her. Plan socially entertaining activities, town fairs, theaters, live shows, walks on the beach, dancing, etc.

She expects for her Prince to have a sense of humor. He needs to be able to make a joke and take a joke, goof around, and laugh often. He needs to be teased like a boy and a girl tease each other when they are children, "dare her to catch the mouse," if you will. She wants to be a "little girl" in a grown up body and wishes for her man to acknowledge this fact and play along.

She wants integrity and loyalty from her man. She expects for her man to keep his promises. She knows that once a man violates his word, she loses admiration and respect for him. It is important for her to know her man belongs to her; and only her.

She wants quality time with her Prince. Quality time involves her and her man investing time together going to the beach, watching a movie, going to the park, chatting over a cup of coffee, walking in the mall, visiting a museum, dancing, vacationing, camping, etc. She knows time is scarce. For this reason, she wants to maximize time doing quality activities with her man.

She wants a conversationalist. To her, a conversationalist is a person capable of listening 80 percent of the time and speaking 20 percent of the time. **Listening is a GIFT we offer to people.** Listening is powerful because it is therapeutic for all of us! When we attentively listen to a speaker, we allow the speaker to vent out feelings, emotions, ideas and concerns. Listening is the vehicle we have to understand people and situations, as well as to guide and control conversations and objectives. Great listeners are not only valuable, but sought out desperately. There are too few of them. Most of the people are talkers, especially women. A man must be a great listener!

A man must be capable of **LISTENING and UNDERSTANING**. He needs to listen well so he can ask appropriate questions with the objective to understand her. Her ideas can be big or small and her conversations lively or boring. She wants an **ATTENTIVE EAR** and the freedom to speak her truth as she sees it without fear. A person willing to be present and non-judgmental of her conversations and ideas. A listener willing to provide constructive feedback when she requests it. No matter how big or small the subject she wants to talk about, she just wants to be listened to and understood by her man.

She expects for her Prince to be confident and support her growth as a woman. In order for a woman to evolve into the person she wants to be, she needs a confident man on her side. She needs an unselfish, mature man. A man of savvy that is not intimidated by her continued growth as a person. The gentleman that will hold her accountable to her word and promises. A friend that will encourage and offer reassurance, trust, and able to turn her incredibility and doubt into a "you can do it" attitude.

She wants to be admired and respected. She takes care of herself physically, make-up well balanced, fresh hairstyle, nicely dressed-up, impeccable shoes, provocative perfumes and aromas. She speaks eloquently. She walks sensually. She is confident in her femininity. She wants men to acknowledge and admire her. However, when she offers her presence or her opinions, she expects for her man to take her seriously. She expects to be respected and treated as a human being and as a woman.

A woman wants her man to be respectful to others and for others to respect him. Garnering respect from her, his friends, family, strangers, and coworkers means the same people, most likely, will give respect to his family as well. This shows her that others value and respect him as an individual. What is even more important to her is that he respects and values others also. No woman wants a "Dodo bird" everyone disrespects. No mature woman wants a bully or a man with a sense of superiority. She wants a mature, centered man. A man that has wisdom and patience. She wants a man who is in control of his life.

She wants to give her **GIFT** to someone worthwhile. Her gift to men is sex. It is the culmination of romance and seduction. Delivering her body, her spirit, her whole being, willingly and without reservation, to a man is the trophy she grants her man for doing a well-done job during the romance and seduction process. Women want and look for men equal or better than them either mentality, spiritually, emotionally, financially. Women want to be with men that are not intimidated or dominated by them. Men with strong character and presence.

Women Crave for 3 Qualities in a Man:

A woman wishes for her man to have 3 qualities: 1. a friend. 2. A husband. 3 A LOVER. Of these three qualities, she wants her man to ALWAYS be a LOVER.

She needs a friend to share time with. A friend willing to listen and talk to. A friend to confide her secrets with openly. Someone she can bond with and have a mutual affection. Someone that is always there for her no matter what. She wants an unconditional friend with her. A friend she can goof-around with and act like a bratty-little girl. She craves a guy strong enough to disagree with her and challenge her position.

She needs a husband who is a leader to follow and surrender to. Someone willing to give her unconditional love. Someone willing and able to provide and share unconditionally. A partner that loves her for what she represents and stands for. A role model she can brag about with her friends.

A LOVER. That's right. A LOVER. She craves to find in her husband a never-ending lover. A fun person to romance and have sex with. A person aware and willing to always court her. Courtship never ends. He is her emotional shelter, her "dirty-boy that freely allows her to be HIS "secret dirty-girl." The guy that breaks her rules in intimacy. The guy that brings excitement into her private and public life. The person that provokes and dares her to express her sensuality, freely, in intimacy. The guy which breaks the monotony and routine of her daily life. She loves having a symbiotic relationship. It is EXTREMELY IMPORTANT FOR MEN TO BE AND ACT AS LOVERS FOR THEIR SPOUSES, **ALWAYS**. Do to her what you would do to her if she was your secret lover. If she was your lover, what would you do to her? What places would you take her? That is what women want! That is what all men should do. She wants that! Give it to her! See what happens!

3

A RIDE

TO

MEMORY LANE

To grasp women, it is extremely important to understand their past history. You see, we cannot improve what we do not understand. In other words, we cannot make a better computer if we do not know why it works the way it does. We cannot become better if we do not know what makes us do what we do. You cannot understand women if you do not understand why they function as they do. We have to comprehend their history.

Why do we need to study women's history? I can tell you this: you will look at women with a more profound meaning and understanding once you conceptualize their history. You will be able to decipher their attitudes and how to handle them. Why they behave as they behave and do what they do! It is fascinating! You will look at them differently.

Back In the Days

Back in the days, a man did not have to work for his woman. It was a man's world. Men forced women to surrender by oppression. Men forced his little girls to only play with little girls. Fathers commanded their boys on the concept of "women were born to serve and obey men". Men work outside the house. Women work inside the house. He kills the animal. She cooks the animal. Men get together with "the boys" after work to drink. Mom cooks and feeds the family and is in charge of the children's upbringing and education. If children turned out bad, men blamed the wife; and he made sure she would hear about it.

Men forced women to respect them. Insubordination from a woman to her man was intolerable by him and society. A woman could not contradict, raise her voice, or maintain eye contact with her husband. Eye contact was a sign of challenge and defiance.

A man could have several women. She could not complain about it. A man would not sleep at his house for days at a time and the woman knew to remain quiet and submissive.

Man made the big decisions. Woman lived with the consequences. She was not allowed to think. Her job was to serve and obey. She was considered incompetent and unqualified. Her point of view did not matter and few looked after them. Some people say they were considered less than human. Go figure!

Men forced women to marry someone they did not love, like, or sometimes even knew. The husband was chosen for her. In many cultures women were, and still are, traded in exchange for money, animals, or land.

Men punished women for abandoning their husbands, even if their husbands turned out to be worthless and/or abusive. There was nothing they could do about it! It was a man's land.

Married Men forced their wives to have intercourse. Wives submitted against their will. Men were not concerned if women achieved orgasms or not. Men sought personal gratification. It was all about him.

I can go on and on with more examples, but I see no reason, you get the point. It was a man's world based on force and oppression. Times changed and a new era for men and women was born: "The Era of Male Feminization and Women Masculinization." Everything changed for both genders.

MALE FEMINIZATION AND FEMALE MASCULINIZATION

Some say it started in 1940 and others assure it started in the 60s. The point is that women and men rebelled against each other and challenged social dogmas and applications of laws. The Era of Male-Feminization and Woman-Masculinization.

The 40s has a lot to do with this social transformation. The United States participated in World-War II. The government sent too many men to war. It depleted man power in the work force. Factories did not have enough man-power to keep up with demand and supply to support an international war and satisfy local necessities for people to survive as a society, food, shelter, etc. Logically, companies hired women to replace men in the work force to satisfy international and local demands. Women woke up early in the morning, left their children at childcare centers, and went to work in factories where man used to work. Women pushed cars, produced parts, operated heavy machinery, got greasy, lifted metal, and so on. They became the man-power at the workplace, earned wages for labor, and became household supporters. They, basically, adopted the responsibilities of the man (and the attitudes, too) and retain the responsibilities as women as well.

For several months or years, women were the sole leaders and providers of the household. Gradually, women became independent. They realized they did not need the support of men to survive. They worked, earned money, and supplied to themselves all life necessities. Men were not needed any more as household providers. So the mentality of "I do not need a man to support me" was born: "Women's Power." Everybody has seen the picture of the woman displaying a bandana on her head, pretty and defiant eyes with a tight fist in front of her pretty face with a dirt-like stain on it, promulgating masculine toughness, as a sign of women's power. This picture became the propaganda of that era.

Women got this "Women's Power" idea out of context. This type of propaganda was created to persuade women to accept jobs at factories originally performed by men. Women felt uncomfortable accepting these "men" positions. They believed these positions were not suitable for women. They were afraid of taking on this challenge. So the government created that powerful picture to motivate women to accept jobs originally performed by men. So they did! The marketing strategy worked!

However, a few women gave a different message to that picture. They used that picture to send an after-war message to the world: "Women's Power." Women started to project male behaviors, became more masculine, aggressive, intimidating, demanding, authoritative even, more of "my way or the highway." Many women converted the "Women's Power" marketing idea into a call for women to initiate a movement to fight for women independence.

When men returned from war, they arrived to houses mostly maintained by women with manly attitudes. Men expected to return to the original routine: setting the family's rules and orders. They did not realize their women had developed a masculine ideology. Women did not put up with their men's demands and orders. Women made it clear to men they had the capacity to work, earn money, and be independent. They really did not need men. If the men would walk out of the house, women would survive without them. When men went to war, women were okay running the house alone. So, if men did not like their women's masculine attitude, women figured, they can leave, we don't need them. Women thought, hey, this guy has not been around the house for a long time, he is not coming into my house to tell me how I have to behave or how things around here need to be done. They discovered they could get the house going with or without a man on their side.

So, men toned down their attitude toward women. They surrendered. When a man raised his voice at his woman, she cut him short by saying: "Hey, I don't need that attitude in my house. Either you tone it down or you will have to leave". Men obeyed. Women demanded more equality from men. Women understood they needed fair treatment from men in order to get alone. After all, they did not need men anymore. Men went along with the idea of "women really do not need men." Men became more submissive and responded with a more feminine attitude.

They fostered a more feminine energy. When women shouted at them, men remained quiet. He did not know how to react. It was best to just avoid the fight. If she was disrespectful to him, he avoided the confrontation under the idea that "she does not know what she is talking about. It is pointless to reason with her". Women found that work, money, and a masculine attitude was a good leverage against men. Men, out of love and sympathy for women, accepted the new women they have found and their new masculine energy. Men returned tired of fighting a war abroad, they were not willing to fight another war in their house. They avoided anything capable of creating conflict just to satisfy their women so they can have peace at home. They played carelessness.

Women saw the power of masculine energy. They enjoyed the "New Me Attitude". Women became the King and Queen of the house. They could do as they pleased. They created a man willing to be controlled by his woman and able to defend her upon her request. They reasoned, when the going gets too tough, they had a man willing to stand up for them at the snap of a finger. More and more, men would become the baby-sitters, diaper changers, home cooks, housemaids, flower keepers, "a house's door mat", if you will.

Women discovered that men can also do the chores that, traditionally, they did and that women can do the activities men traditionally did. Thus, the new era of Male-Feminization and Female-Masculinization was born. The actual beginnings of men-women "equality." This attitude gradually influenced women around the globe. Women around the world began craving the freedoms of the "American Women".

The 1960s were the carry-over results from the post-war "Women's Power" Era. My friend heard a story from a leader of a hippie camp and how the "Let's Burn the Bra" Era continue with the Male-Feminization and Female-Masculinization movement. Here it is:

Brother A and Brother B sat down on a porch to converse about work, money, women, fun, while smoking pot near San Francisco, CA. Brother A, in a moment of hallucination, had a realization. He tells Brother B how fulfilling it would be to just quit his job and never work again, devalue money and just be free, have a lot of fun with alcohol, pot and girls. Brother B likes the idea. He asks Brother A how they can go about making that realization happen. Brother A did not know at the time, but promised to think about it. They smoked more pot and continue to talk about how to make that realization happen.

Finally, one pot smoking day, they found their answer: start a social movement. Brother A says to Brother B he wants to be free. Free from all responsibilities. He is going to live his life to its fullest. He is going to start a social movement. Brother B asked Brother A what would be the cause for the movement. Brother A said his cause will be for men and women equality.

He explains to Brother B that women were just as equal as men. If a man can smoke pot, then she should be allowed to smoke pot with them without fear of judgment. If a man can take his shirt off publically, then a woman should be able to take her shirt off as well. If men can party, a woman should be able to party. If men drink, women should drink. Men don't use make-up, women should have the right to not use make-up. Men are self-dependent, women should be independent. If men and women are independent, then they don't need the each other nor a government. If we don't need the government, then we don't have to pay taxes. We don't want to pay taxes, let's not work. We don't need to work to buy food because we will cultivate our own food. We don't need the big cities, we will create our own community. Next thing you know, you and I will have exactly what we want: plenty of women, lots of pot, lots of fun, lots of people to harvest food and cook for us, lots of land, and we do not even have to work for it. We just need to get a group of pissed-off, reveled teenagers, sell them the idea, they will do the rest. And so, it happened. Next thing you know, teenagers created one the largest social movements causing global impact. This attitude gradually influenced women around the globe. Again, women around the world wanted to be like the "American Women".

Rethinking the Hippie Era

It took women a little time to figure out that they were treated as pleasurable objects during the Hippie times. Women went into the movement for "equality and freedom" and found themselves being abused and mistreated. Men became jobless, vagabonds, unable to provide for or protect women. Men used women to provide for their own survival. Their women went along with the idea. Women earned the money, food, shelter, and clothing for men. They thought that by providing and supporting men they would move closer to equality. Men found that it was a way for them to lazy around, smoke pot, eat, have sex and relax. All for free! A dream come true for men. They loved it!

Women wanted to be just like man. What do men want? The opportunity to have sex with multiple partners, like a bee going from flower to flower. So, men did not have to work that much to find a partner and have sex. Since women were open to have sex with any man, women facilitated the effort for men to live in paradise. In essence, the flower went from bee to bee. This was paradise for men and women at first.

But too much is too much. As expected, women got tired of men taking advantage of them. They got tired of having a lazy men on their side, feminine men unwilling to provide for them or claim their women. Women gradually understood they were heading in the wrong direction: too much sex, drugs, and too little money. I can only imagine the feeling of a woman falling in love with a man, knowing his man is penetrating multiple gals and she is well aware of it, and she has to eat her pride and feelings just to keep "the movement" going. It was awful.

Women hated the idea of miscarriages and abortions. Sleeping in one place tonight and waking up at another place tomorrow. They hated the fact they had to deal with all types of sexually transmitted diseases. They were not valued as women. They could not take the fact that they were not special anymore. They were common and ordinary, disposable sexual toys, if you will. They were not happy at all! So, they set out to reinvent themselves and become special again, to regain pride in being feminine and a woman. This attitude gradually influenced women around the planet. Newly, women around the universe wanted to be like "American Women".

Male Feminization - Female Masculinization and Hollywood

Hollywood has played a major part in transforming or, I should better say, confusing men and women, let alone families as a whole, worldwide regarding the roles of men and women. Shows, movies and programming aired via television have, BIG TIME, influenced human behavior universally. Look at the programming nowadays played on television and movies. Pay special attention to the embedded messages projected by actors and presentations. "Married with Children," "Everybody Loves Raymond," "The King of Queens," and many more do a pretty good job shaping people's idea about the position of men and women in our current society. Men are portrayed as dumb, incapable, lazy, idiots, villains, ruffians, selfish, house cleaners, baby sitters, un-trustable, useless, idle, feckless, stupid, goofy, clownish, sloppy, you name it, and it has been done.

Movies portray men in the same fashion as TV does, just in a more romantic way ("Lier, Lier" "Couples Retreat," "Grown-ups," "Forest Gump," etc...). They show men as needy, unmotivated, desperate, hopeless, skirt-chasers, cry-babies, cowards, afraid, weak-hearted, unreliable, not well-rounded, bad lovers, softies, irrelevant, un-necessary, failures, follower, submissive, dependent, and I can go on and on and won't finish with the list.

Cartoons do just as good belittling men. Peepa Pig's dad for some reason or another is always the butt of the jokes. NEMO's dad is a coward clown fish with low self-esteem problems. The Simpsons speaks for itself. Never mind the "American Dad." You name the show and most likely, you will find male feminization at stake.

Television, movies and cartoons portray women in the opposite way as they portray men. Macho-like, ALPHA, intelligent, the heroine, all-powerful, the king of the house, the defender, the conqueror, the leader. You want more, just read the paragraphs above this one and turn them around and think the opposite of those words. That's Hollywood assigning new roles for women and men. We buy these roles and then, we sell them to our children.

Our children watch TV and movies daily. They adopt the embedded messages projected by the actors and actresses. Their inexperienced and immature minds can be easily influenced. Boys grow up thinking that it is okay to project female energies and behave like girls. The girls grow up thinking that it is their right to behave like a men and project a masculine energy. I have never seen so many men and women, in my many years of life, dating and marrying members of the same sex. I am not against homosexuality. You do with yourself and your body whatever makes you happy.

My point is this. How can we expect our girls to be attracted to wimpy, female-like, needy men? And how can we expect for men to be attracted to women when women think the worst of them and treat them as disposable? How can we not expect a 60 percent divorce rate when two confused people get married and play equivocal roles? How can we not expect our youth to find happiness in drugs and alcohol when they live a faulty, sad reality? How can we expect for our children to change the world when the role models they admire live a life of gossip, problems, frustrations, envy, vanity, based on lives invented by Hollywood writers and producers? Shouldn't we look at our parents as role models to emulate because they execute their roles as a man and woman effectively and with integrity? We have assigned the parental responsibility and our children's education to Hollywood. And we expect our children to outperform children in the world. We give our boys and girls roles they cannot mentally conceive and are rare to them. No wonder kids nowadays are growing up angry and stressed out early in life. And we as parents, blame everything and everyone for our own short comings as men and women. Hollywood has done its part in disfiguring men and women alike and, so have we, as men and women, by approving and allowing, Hollywood's influence in our home. Men have allowed media to be the leader in their house. They have done quite well and we are paying the price for it.

There is a great trend happening slowly, though. Many men and women have desired to take back control of family standards. Men want to be men again. Women want to be women again. Men and women have learned that they can have their cookie and eat it, too. A new movement has started! I call it the "Women Appreciation Movement."

WOMEN APPRECIATION MOVEMENT

5

WOMEN
APPRECIATION
MOVEMENT

The cause of this new movement has to do with women appreciation. They want to be valued again as women. They don't want to be subdued to men's dictatorship or be treated as a sexual object. They want to be guided not controlled by men; they already had too much of that; they are tired of it. It is like the kid who can freely eat candy at the candy store. Eventually, he will eat too much of it and will become disgusted by it. He will then want something new and exciting. Just like the kid, women want something new and exciting. They expect for men to be men, again! Woman expect men to have grown mentally, just as they have.

Women demand more of themselves now days. They project the opposite behavior they showed during the Hippie Era. They project more class and elegance. They compete for beauty and display more feminine, sculptured bodies. They walk provocatively. Women, today, take the time to groom themselves with proper make-up applications and artful hair styles. They are fresh and smell good, get waxing done, wear sensual lingerie, with colorful and elegant pedicures and manicures and tasteful clothing. Their cars and houses mimic their personalities and tastes.

Today's women are more assertive, confident, and independent. Some are career oriented. Others, family oriented. They are more happy, astute, social and more open-minded. Too many of them are very competitive and goal oriented. They represent value. However, women have become pickier in selecting men. They expect for men to be at least equal but would prefer a higher scale. They see themselves as something special, again.

They expect for men to behave as men. They want a man who values his word and is of character. Someone who is decisive, goal-oriented, understanding, a great listener, attentive, and confident. A man a woman can count on. A man who is knowledgeable and capable to lead them. They expect a man in the family, a great partner and a male example for children. They also want common sense men with experience on how to treat them as women and men willing to romance and seduce them. Finally, they desire men with strong principles and values. A man, strong enough and capable to penetrate them spiritually, emotionally, and physically.

Of course, women want men to be well-groomed and also take care of their body and be physically fit, dresses appropriately, neatly manicured hands and toe nails, hygienic and smells good. As you can see by now, women have elevated their expectations for themselves and for men in their lives.

EARN YOUR WOMAN

Nowadays, men are expected to EARN their women. IF they want a woman on their side, they have to work hard for her. That means, investing time, energy, and money, a lot of money. Fast talking will not cut it. Romance-express will not do it. Immediate seduction is history. Sex on the spot, a thing of the past. No more freebees. The era of forced relationships and female oppression has long past. Women have developed stronger expectations for themselves and from men. Again, women expect for men to invest resources on them, lots of resources.

Little girls are now allowed to play with boys. Boys are taught to respect and protect women. Daddy tells Jr. that it is okay for a man to take care of the interior of the house while Mom makes a living as well. Both parents hold each other accountable for the education and upbringing of the children. Both parents are to blame if the children turn out unsuccessful.

Men must EARN a woman's respect nowadays. It is okay now for a woman to contradict her man, raise her voice to express her opinion freely, look at men dead in the eye and challenge them. Women no longer accept her man to have multiple women. He must come back to sleep in his house daily or he will not hear the end of it.

Men are hunters now. If he wants a woman, he needs to find her on his own. A man must EARN a woman's trust before she can commit to anything, let alone marriage. Yeah, a man must work for his woman. Women have too many choices nowadays, on both sides of the fence. They are choosers now. It is considered okay for a woman to leave a partner that turned out to be a bad partner.

Men are allowed by women to make the big decision; as long as their point of view is taken into consideration. Women want to share consequences with men. Our society considers that women are competent to make sound decisions. Her job is to participate in the thinking and doing process. Her opinion matters.

Men must EARN sex with women. Women want you to romance and seduce them. She will have sex with a man, but on her own terms and once the man has EARNED her gift. This attitude spilled gradually and influenced women around the world just like before.

You get the point with these examples. A MAN MUST WORK FOR HIS WOMAN NOWADAYS. Let me tell you a story to help you understand the men and women of today.

6

MEN AND DOGS

We all know a Dog could be a man's best friend. It all depends on how you treat the dog and who is watching. The dog will tolerate corporal and malnutrition abuse. He won't abandon his master; until someone else shows up and provides the dog with appreciation, a home, food, affection, and love. When this happens, little by little, the dog starts to detach from its original owner and begins developing comfort with the new provider. The original master needs to shape up and deliver the dog's needs, if not, gradually, the dog starts to follow and be with him less and less, until the dog decides to leave his master, permanently.

If the dog gets its needs met at its house, there is nothing to worry about. The dog has no need to look in the streets for what he already has at home. He is not going anywhere. However, if his master does not provide the dog's necessities, it is a matter of time before the dog finds another love, another woman.

As long as the dog's needs are fulfilled, he will stick around with his partner, puppies, and the house. If a dog has something good going on in its house, the dog is very protective and loving. The dog protects and guards its home and territory, its female companionship, and their puppies. Dogs are unselfish and willing to sacrifice themselves for a great cause or worthwhile person.

Dogs love sex. They are not in the game of romanticism but are willing to court its partner if the end result is sex. If he does not get what he needs with his partner, he will find it somewhere else. If his fantasies are not satisfied at home, someone else will satisfy them. It is that simple.

A dog has special, God-given qualities and strengths that should not be ignored. Dogs are indispensable in any society. Dogs like to fight and protect. Unlike cats that like to tease and hide. Don't forget this little, but very important fact: Not to ignore a dog or take it for granted.

Dogs are trusting animals. However, once that trust is violated, the dog carries the scar with him for life. Dogs have the memory of an elephant. Let's not forget dogs have feelings, too. They express those feelings by either barking or expressing happy emotions (jumping, playing happily around, and so on). I saw a dog whining and crying over the tombstone of its deceased master. That's how much a dog can love, just like a man.

Dogs aim for the bite. No beating around the bush. If anyone tries to invade its territory, the dog will react and defend. They are adrenaline driven. Dogs do not look for the touchy-touchy feeling, like cats. They cannot be or act feminine. They act masculine because that is their God-given nature.

Every dog needs liberty. It needs to be able to wonder and sniff around. They like to explore territories. This is how the dogs discover new opportunities. This is their way of building self-esteem, confidence and strength. Free dogs are happy dogs. However, when dogs are restricted, and punished physically or emotionally, and their freedom prohibited, they turn into unhappy dogs, develop low self-esteem, and quickly snap into aggressive behaviors, a threat to others around him. They will bite.

Dogs have the wonderful attribute of being patient since birth. Unfortunately, the daily experiences of life, business, children, friends, and its master determine the dog's behavior. If the partner or master suffer from tension, pressure, stress, fear, negativity then the dog will live a life mimicking its master's behaviors and fears. The dog is always serene when not exposed to these factors.

Just like a dog needs a strong, energy-compatible master, so do men need a woman compatible to his view of life and expectations. Men's and dogs' behavior have a lot in common

7

WOMEN AND CATS

I remember visiting the house of a woman. I knocked on the door and she opened it. I gained entrance into her house. I noticed from a far distance, there was a cat studying me carefully. I felt as if I was a sniper's target. I asked the woman if the cat had any problems with stranger visiting her home. She said "No". She assured me that the cat was timid and, actually, very loving. He will be okay once it becomes familiar with me. She commented her cat was like her.

I walked into her living room. I noticed the cat kept on watching me. It walked side to side and around the house perusing me. It circumambulated me in the same fashion as a Lion circles a prey. It vacillated with the idea of coming or not coming toward me to touch him. I thought the cat was a little odd. It looked at me. Walked. Stopped. Wandered around pretending to ignore me. He performed this ritual several times. I did not pay much attention to it. I kept on chatting with the pretty lady.

I, suddenly, realized the cat was about 6 inches in front of me. It looked at me. I thought the cat wanted to smell me. The cat seemed timid and afraid. I asked the woman if the cat was okay with me being there. She smiled and nodded her head up and down. She told me the cat was just trying to size me up, to get to know me; that was all. It is teasing you. It wants to know what kind of a man you are. Once it feels secure, it will approach you. I smiled at her. Two minutes later, I felt the cat rubbing the right side of its body against my calf muscle on my right leg, demanding my attention. I looked at the cat, smiled, and continued my conversation with the woman. The cat walked away from me. It did not care for my lack of attentions. It returned to its original location.

I continued my conversation with the lady. 5 minutes later, I felt the cat pushing and rubbing its body against my same leg again. Its spinal cord curled upwards, as if an invisible hand was pulling the top of its fur toward the living room ceiling. It lifted up its tail as well. I ignored its presence. The cat walked away from me, again. This time, it did not retract to the original location. This time it stayed around its master. It wandered around her and kept on touching me, then walked away from us.

She invited me over to sit down on the sofa. The cat made its appearance, again. The cat made an effort to win my attention, again. It is testing me. The cat made its way in between the front of the sofa and my calves. I reached for the cat to caress its body and the cat walked away from me really fast. The woman suggested for me not to pay much attention to the cat. The cat was trying to size you up and get to know you better. *She told me that cats and women do that.* They look at you first with curiosity, becomes interested, teases with you and, once they feel secure, they become approachable and would let you touch them, ultimately, they will offer you their body. I became more interested in this cat than in the conversation with the woman. The tables turned around! Now, I was the Dog studying the cat! How bizarre, how bizarre?

The cat approached me again. This time, I was able to touch it more and caress it. Its head made its way under my fingertips. Its body shook and twisted as if the cat was having an orgasm. It was rare. Then, all of a sudden, walked away. I stood up from the sofa to grab and hug him. It ran away from me. I tried chasing it. The more I chased the cat, the more difficult it became to grab him. I quitted chasing the cat. I figured it made no sense to befriend a cat unwilling to cooperate. I returned to sit down on the sofa, again.

While sitting down on the sofa, I felt the cat rubbing its body against the back of my head. It demanded my attention, again. I tried touching him and the cat almost retrieved from me. I kept calm and ignored the cat, as if being indifferent. The cat became more comfortable and made its way onto my lap. The cat rested there. I massaged its body and the cat seemed to have fallen asleep. I removed the cat from me twice. I placed it on the floor so it walk away. It came back for more love and care. How bizarre. How bizarre.

Who understands this cat, I mentioned to the lady. Not long ago, the cat did not want anything to do with me. I caress it and it walks away, I chased it and it runs away. I don't make a move to show interest on it and here it is, sleeping on my lap, completely at my disposal. Odd, isn't it?

Women are like cats. They demand attention and vacillate too much. They will test you to size you up to discover the caliber of a man you are. They walk around, run away, and behave indifferent to build up momentum and gain importance. They are manipulative and opportunistic. They like to tease men to test their strength and self-control level. They do this ritual to make sure a man is comfortable with his skin and core as a male. Once they "figure" men out and they feel secure and comfortable, they will fall asleep on your lap, surrendering their body, completely. Only then, they would allow men to penetrate them spiritually, emotionally, and physically.

You have a better understanding on women and men by now. It is time for us to move to the core of the relationship. Why relationships work as they do. How to make them better and in the process become better people ourselves.

The world of energies within a relationship. You are about to change your world and your paradigm. You are about to transform and reengineer yourself. You are about to undertake a journey that will change the way you view women and men in a relationship and the way you perceive yourself. More importantly, you will identify how to be a better human being and a more effective lover and partner. Social dogmas and parental teachings will be challenged. Be ready. Your transformation is about to begin.

8

THE SECRET ENERGIES: ALPHA BETA GAMA

By far, the greatest discovery you will make during this odyssey will be discovering the world of energies: The world of ALPHAs, BETAs, and GAMAs. A massive and potent nugget of wisdom capable of transforming lives and societies. Those who take the time to learn, comprehend, and apply these energies, experience more tranquil and controlled relationships. They become more serene and savvy themselves. They do so because from the begging, they pick the right energy.

I grew up thinking that just because I was born male I was a man. A woman born as a woman was a woman. Society has set certain behavioral expectations for men and women. Men take care of women and women take care of men and both take care of children. My parents told me I was stronger than women, at least physically. As a man, I had the responsibility to take care of women, especially, of my female partner. In return, women owed me respect and submission. No matter what type of quality of life and the type of man I was in a relationship, I deserved the respect of women. I did not have to invest any effort on becoming a better man. Why? Women would respect me either as a good or bad man. I entered into relationships using this approach. Too many people followed this pattern and doctrine as I did. We believed it was the "right way to go" because it was promulgated socially and approved by our parents. What a learning experience! It was the wrong approach. This doctrine and approach has lead too many people to build the house's foundation on loose sand. The wrong way to select a woman. The wrong way to build a fruitful and successful relationship. The right way to failure.

Then, I ran across the wonderful world of ALPHAs, BETAs, and GAMAs. I discovered this world right about the time my 2nd relationship had collapsed, badly. It caught my attention from the beginning. I knew I had found something BIG! Something special and spectacular! I was correct. I had found the way to decipher my past relationships and the reason for their failure. I found a way to decipher myself, too! I, also, identified the world of energies as the MAIN tool to better select partners, friends, build stronger relationships, and a fulfilling life. These energies came to me at the right time. At a moment when I needed to understand why my relationships ended and the reason for their termination. Since I was serious about reinventing myself, I made it my purpose to master this world of energies. I studied them profoundly to deep comprehension. I applied them until I reached success with them multiple times. They worked. I shared these energies with other people; they worked as well! I know they will work for you, too. Don't take my word for it. Try them yourself. However, DO NOT apply them until you profoundly comprehend them. When you do decide to apply them, apply them with seriousness and be strict about them.

Do you know how to keep secrets? Here is one: ADVICE: Do not tell anyone you are trying to identify what type of energy you or they have: ALPHA, BETA, or GAMA.

This re-engineering process is personal. You don't need anyone to discourage you from your personal reinvention. No one needs to know about it. Operate under the radar. Also, when you start to study people, do so mentally and keep it to yourself. By the same token, no one likes to be studied and deciphered for qualification as a friend or significant other. THIS IS PERSONAL. KEEP IT TO YOURSELF. Once you decipher a person, do not tell them you know what kind of energy they have. THEY DO NOT NEED TO KNOW WHAT TYPE OF ENERGY THEY PROJECT. HOWEVER, YOU MUST KNOW IT!

One last comment on energy application. Once you understand how to decipher people by using the power of energies, your wisdom will spill over to other areas of your life: Identifying the correct acquaintances, friends, supervisors, associates, interviewers, business partners, businesses, almost anyone or anything. These energies are meaningful and powerful. A well-kept secret. AGAIN. KEEP THE DECIPHERING PROCESS AND RESULTS CONFIDENTIAL AND PERSONAL. Let's move on to study and comprehend these energies. Your transformation starts here.

From this moment forward, I will use the words man and woman very little. I will use instead the words ALPHA (Masculine energy), BETA (Feminine energy), GAMA (ALPHA/BETA energy) heavily. These are the words you need to use to decipher a person to identify his or her energy type. Become very familiar with them.

ALPHA ENERGY

ALPHA energy is a masculine energy. A male is expected to have the ALPHA energy. However, this ideal expectation does not actually occur automatically. A man can be ALPHA. A woman can be ALPHA. ALPHA energy commands and leads in a relationship. It does not matter if the man is a man or a woman is a woman. What matters is who calls the shots in the relationship. An ALPHA is always a leader. The leader could be a male or female. A Person can develop an ALPHA energy upon making the decision to become an Alpha.

How do you identify or become an ALPHA? Let me share this ALPHA characteristics with you. An ALPHA:

1. Knows who he is and is comfortable with himself. He has conquered himself. He is the same person everywhere and anytime. He is brave and confident. He understands himself spiritually, emotionally, psychologically and physically. He knows how far he can go on anything he conceives and does. He knows what he expects from others and others expect from him. His hand shake is always firm and conveys strength and confidence.

2. He loves life. He nurtures and projects his inner peace. He sees everything in life as an opportunity to have fun and relax. He makes out of the mundane something special. He possesses and manages well his high-level self-esteem.

3. He is a centered person. A mature person. He is peaceful. Truthful to others and to himself. Always keeps his composure. He always looks for the center when dealing with growth or adversity. He controls situations. He knows how to keep everything neutral and in equilibrium. He thinks before he talks. He keeps his feet on the ground. Knows how to identify the wrong and right paths.

4. He knows what he wants and how he is going to get it. If the challenge is large or small, he makes the challenge manageable. He is focused on his objective. He can identify the roads to follow to reach his mission. He protects his accomplishments.

5. He is intelligent and values intelligence. He is stimulated by ideas, thoughts, concepts, processes, systems, etc.

6. He is energetic. He is almost never tired. He is a fire ball. Always excited. He is always ready to take on the next project.

7. He is goal, purpose, mission, and results-oriented. He promotes growth. He always knows what he expects from his challenges. He wants to conquer the world. He is a die-hard. No matter how many times he tries, he won't quit. He does not sacrifice his dream or goals for no one or anything and is willing to defend them.

8. He cares for himself, first. He is well groomed and takes care of his body. Exercises often and eats appropriately to keep fit and attractive. Always dresses appropriately for the occasion. His hair is modern and neatly done. Very hygienic. Smells good all the time. His apparel is well balanced in color and design. His image is important to him.

9. He controls by leading. A natural leader. Either born or made. They solve problems. They live by high morals, principles and values. They measure others by morals, principles and values. Others look for him to give them direction and confidence. He possess highly developed social skills. He allows others to express their concerns and lead them to find the results.

10. He hangs out most of the time solo. He values his time. He leans on himself for life challenges. When hanging out with others, he hangs around

other ALPHAs; preferable more accomplished ALPHAS.

ALPHA Body Language

1. They walk slowly with long, measured steps, looking toward the distance, as if having mental binoculars. Every step they take is carefully calculated and firm. Arms and hands swinging freely on the sides. They are not in a hurry, even if they are off schedule. They are tranquil, controlled, and smooth drivers. They eat their food, closed mouth, and swallow slowly. They turn their head and body slowly. They approach everything in a slow, controlled, calculated motion.
2. The Mysterious Alpha.
    - They Listen. Understand. Ask questions to clarify or to continue the discovery process 80 percent of the time. They share vague personal information 10 percent of the time to allow the discovery process to remain a mystery, fun and thrilling. They are witty 10 percent of the time.
    - They are Secretive. They don't boast what they do with women or others. Although others might brag about what they do, when questioned, ALPHAs favorite reply is: "I am sorry, I have a bad memory". Thus, he remains mysterious. Stays completely out of gossip.

- Alphas treat every woman the same. All women are the same. Therefore none of them deserve special treatment. They grasp the fact that a woman wants to be appreciated by her internal beauty, not as a beautiful trophy. ALPHAs do not place women on pedestals, they see them eye-to-eye.
- Mysterious ALPHAs conceal feelings and emotions. Unclear feeling and emotions create curiosity and attraction.
- They have the temperament to consume alcohol to enhance an enjoyable moment controllably. They do not consume alcohol to get wasted and disgusting. They see their bodies as temples, therefore, drugs are out of the question. They also do not hang around people unable to match their temperament and expectation when having fun.
- A mysterious man is hard to get. He takes his time to get to know the person. He is a master in creating tension, attraction, and identifying chemistry; and he takes his time to do so. He does not spend the night with someone on the first date. Although, ALPHAs find pleasure on the courtship process, they are cautious, they make sure the person they are with meet their expectations and deserve them. They are

always willing to walk-away from a deal, no matter how good it is.

- They are independent. They can sustain themselves financially and emotionally. He can endure difficult financial times. They are happy with or without someone on their side. They are stable and sustainable.
- A Loner. They find in solitude peace, harmony, personal discovery and understanding. In isolation, they find the arena they need to analyze and dissect the complexities of the world and their strategy to tackle it. When they are apart from others, they find the opportunity to comprehend people and themselves. Solo, he formulates ideas, goals, and concepts. They use this time to "sell the dream" to themselves. Although it seems they are not accompanied, they are not really desolated. They are always in the company of their goals, wishes, desires, plans, ideas, energies, and their willingness to have a meaningful purpose, a reason for their time on this earth. By being detached from the world, they find meaningful reasons for their existence and the existence of others. In solitary periods, they locate their strengths and weaknesses, their opportunities and disadvantages. In silence, they can absorb the world without interruption. It is during these

quiet, lonely times, that they develop the desires and courage to handle the world alone.

- ALPHAs do not chase; they do not need to. They don't chase women, businesses, friends, or anyone to be accepted, appreciated and valued. They know who they are and what they represent to others. He does not invade, bother, or become obnoxious with over texting, emailing, phone calling, messaging, or by becoming a pest or a stalker. They are not needy nor do they need obsessive attention from others to remain centered and appreciated. They are indifferent.

And, talking about indifference, I am going to interject an EXTREMELY valuable nugget of information I received from Smithy, the person that introduced me to the concept of indifference. A make-you or break-you concept. Smithy is a "Ladies Man."

He said, "Indifference has been heavily undervalued, Alfredo. Yet, the concept of indifference, is a supreme factor. So mighty, it can make you or break you. I can mold you into a weak or a solid person. Indifference is the condiment that can turn platinum to rubber or rubber into platinum. It is that paramount! Yet, so simple and, as such, we take it for granted; men specially. And those who understand it, keep the secret only for themselves".

Tell me more, Smithy, I demanded, "Pay attention, boy, what I am about to tell you can change your life for good or for bad. Here we go..." he said. "Indifference is a SUPREME factor because it challenges a person to wrestle with psychological and emotional punches inflicted by others. The fight is within yourself, in your guts and brain. It is a fight that either you or the person inflicting the punches of indifference must win. Stamina and skill will determine if you would lose or win. It all depends on how you handle indifference from others to you and indifference from you to others. There is ONLY one outcome, you win or you lose. The good or bad thing about this fight is that once the fight is over, you keep the results. Do you understand", Smithy asked me. "Somewhat", I replied.

"Let me give an example", Smithy proposed. "You see a woman you like and you approach her. You say "hello" and she ignores you. How do you take her rejection? "I would try again," I replied. "NOOOO", he said. "You don't take the rejection personal. Even though, you feel angry, emotionally disappointed, and psychologically confused, you don't take it personal and you don't try again and again and again. She will perceive you as needy and inexperienced. Women hate this attitude, boy! Besides, you owe respect to yourself. You don't allow her rejection to overpower your brain and your gut. Don't pay attention to her anymore, ignore her, and move on. If she likes you she will try to regain your attention. If she does not like you, she will ignore you all day long, boy! *And you should not care either way*! *You should be the same happy person with or without her.* Get it?" he boasted.

"Here is another example", said Smithy. "You text your friend a simple "Hello, Kathy" and, you know she received your text message. Your friend doesn't reply back or simply replies at an unreasonable time. What do you do?" he asked? "I send another text..." I replied unsure about my answer. "NOOO," he complained. "You don't! Your phone will tell you if your message did not go through, isn't that right?" he inquired. "Yes," I answered. "If it doesn't go through then text again. However, if it did, then don't text again. Think ping-pong. You send the little ball to the other side. You, then, wait until the other side sends you back the ball.

Don't chase! Don't beg! Don't ask! Don't cry! Don't complain. Don't take it personal! Go about your business. You know she received the message. If she replies, great! If not, great! Life continues. You owe respect to yourself, boy! You don't allow anyone to control your brain and your emotions by ignoring you. You continue with your life as the happy person you are with or without your friend. Si comprende?" he verified. Smithy finished by saying that "The Supreme power of indifference is a relationship tool you must master. Without mastering it, you are as good as a fried potato! Use it as a tool to gain value and relevance. You can use it for private and public use. Women love it because that's how they pinpoint the rubber from metal, needy versus desirable, mature versus inexperience, secure versus insecure. Once women feel your indifference, they start to chase you; they want to chase you because you become interesting. Being indifferent does not mean arrogance, it means confidence!" "Buddy", Smithy asked, "**Want attention? Don't give attention**. This is how you become mysterious and interesting. Don't surrender to women's indifference. If they ignored you, you ignore them as well. If they are indifferent, be indifferent. If you are a great catch, let them miss the catch. Do this and watch what happens," he concluded.

3. ALPHAs are Great Communicators. They have the ability to communicate verbally and non-verbally. They always carry a smile that communicates humility and confidence. When they laugh, everybody hears them, they own the ability to laugh freely. They are not afraid to speak their mind publically and privately. ALPHAs are vivid story tellers. They have the ability to dumb-down complex situations. They use simple words effectively to deliver difficult messages. They are maestros of the concept of: "statistics tell and stories sale". They persuade and make points with real life stories. People can grasp real personal stories more attentively and with more interest. They project and transfer information in a controlled, tranquil, and peaceful manner. It is important to them the recipients of his message understand his message without a doubt. As a slow-talker, he projects and is perceived as a person of wisdom, maturity, respect, understanding, experience, control, and command. They use this knowledge as a strategy to advance their purpose effectively.

They are great listeners. They interact really well in public and in private. People cannot get enough of their attention and presence. Whether they are interacting with people while sitting down or while standing up, they always display confidence, peace, and understanding. They stand up straight, shoulders and body pushed back a little, and in a relaxed mode. Their breathing is calmed, smooth and quite. Stay in contact with speaker while talking or listening. They focus on the topic on hand with the intent to understand. They always ask quality questions to make the conversation more profound. They express disagreements by posing carefully, well thought-out and persuasive questions, in a cool manner, with the intent to guide and educate. If they do not know something, they are always open to explore new knowledge. They are masters of the term: "agree to disagree". People cannot get enough of their stories and are enchanted by their ability to be balance disagreements. Anyone who has interacted with an ALPHA will tell you how pleasant it is to share quality time with a person filled with wisdom and has an attentive, non-judgmental, ear. ALPHAs are great personal growth promoters and they live by it.

4. They are witty. Basically, they possess the ability to think on their toes. They say and write things that are clever and usually funny. For instance, they may say to a child unwilling to brash her teeth the following: "you only brash the teeth you want to keep." They can be comical without showing any emotions or facial expression.

That's what I can tell you about the ALPHA world. Becoming an ALPHA is a matter of making a decision to be one. The same is true for BETAs.

BETA Energy

BETA energy is a feminine energy. A woman is expected to have the BETA energy. However, this ideal expectation does not occur automatically. A man can be BETA. A woman can be BETA. BETA energy submits and follows in a relationship. It does not matter if the man is a man or a woman is a woman. What matters is that BETAs provide the emotional factor in the relationship. A BETA is always a follower. The follower could be male or female. A Person can develop BETA energy upon making the decision to become a submissive, emotional follower.

How do you identify or become a BETA? Let me share these BETA characteristics with you. A person has BETA energy when he or she is:

1. Needy: They always chase; even if they have been rejected multiple times. They over call, over text, over email, over pursue others just to be accepted, gain attention, and be considered. Always looking for compassion and understanding from others.
2. An Approval seeker: Before making decisions, they consult with countless people just to make sure others will be okay with their decision.

3. Submissive: They comply with and follow instructions and orders according to expectations. They are too timid to defend themselves or express their opinion openly when they disagree with the proposition at hand.
4. Indecisive: They have a hard time accepting responsibility to provide results. They stretch time because they lack the ability to make decision quickly effectively. They suffer from *brain-paralysis*; too much analysis... no action!
5. Untrustworthy. They don't keep their promises, dreams and goals. They do not honor their word and place little value to the word of others. They regard integrity as too rigid and authoritative. They say one thing and do something else. They always talk big-game plans because that is how they acquire their adrenaline rushes.

6. Loud and obnoxious: By being loud they believe they would win attention, intimidate, and gain respect from others. They release their frustrations by venting out their stresses and frustrations with people less threatening. When serious problems arise, they scream, offend, hide, threaten or run away. Solving problems rationally is not normal for them. They solve problems emotionally.
7. Dependent: They feel lost and abandoned if they are by themselves. They always depend on the company

of someone to find meaning in their lives and to feel more secure. They believe other people have the responsibility to make them happy. They do not plan or are organized. They don't act, they react. They want others to do all the thinking and planning for them. They just want to enjoy the ride.

8. Low Self-Esteem: They are timid and afraid. They rarely take first-hand risks. They want to avoid failure. They wait for someone else to go first. They take any criticism as negative compliments or personal attacks.

9. Emotional: They get angry quickly if they are not touched, kissed, hugged, disregarded, etc. They are melodramatic. They don't care if they are in public or in private to act child-like.

10. Gossip-driven: Gossiping about other people and their lives is how they find flavor in their own lives. They derive too much pleasure from chatting and sharing with friends private secrets from others or from themselves. Disclosing this type of information is thrilling for them. They live by and mimic the most current reality shows on TV and magazines.

11. Confused: They change directions on almost everything they propose. So much that they become demoralized due to their own confusion.

12. Complainers: Complain about their work, the weather, the traffic, their friends, and just about anything. If they do not get their way, they complain

all day. Not only do they complain, but also they tell the world about it. They cry about their difficult life. They have a different complain every day. When they make a mistake, they are never at fault.

13. They believe in luck. They believe that people are born lucky or with the right tools at their disposal and that is the reason why they are successful. They live in a world of wishful thinking. I wish for this, I wish for that, I wish for the other, on and on.
14. Fantasy world: Expect unrealistic expectations. They expect for others to behave in a way that mimics TV shows, movies, romance novels, and magazines. They live in their own soap opera.
15. Desperate: They feel the sky will fall if they do not get fast enough what they want.

There are many more traits you can use to identify a BETA person. However, I am only identifying the most common and most important right here. How do you identify a BETA's body language? Here we go:

BETA Body Language

1. They walk fast and timidly, as if they are afraid to disturb and incommode people.
2. Eye contact: They avoid eye contact. The eyes vacillates between the floor and the distance,

wondering around as if looking for something. The speaker imposes its presence and BETA submits.

3. Body posture. They stand in a timid position with slouched shoulders. Head down, looking afraid and tired. Rubbing hands; sometime sweaty palms. Move their weight side to side.
4. Fake smiles. Their smiles are not genuine, but rather timid and shy, mechanical, if you will.
5. They keep track of time too close. They look at the clock, watch, or ask people for the time consistently. They are always in a hurry. They always get to appointments late.
6. When talking, they touch their head, chin, arms, face, fidget with small objects as a form of distraction, pick lint off clothes, and narrow their eyes.

GAMA Energy

When we mix ALPHA and BETA energies, we get: GAMA Energy. GAMA energy is a combination of all the qualities and characteristics of male and female attitude. A man or a woman can have, behave, and foster GAMA energy. GAMAs are one type of person in public and a different type of person in private. For example, a person can display all the characteristics of an ALPHA in public and behave BETA in their privacy of their home, or the other way around. They can be BETA in public and ALPHA at home. We all have seen very goal-oriented, aggressive and competitive businessmen on TV, movies, books, and in our personal lives. They are over-achievers. They do not take any BS from any anyone. They are untied tigers.

However, once they arrive home, they become a docile cat. Obedient and submissive. Display feminine characteristics. They have difficulties making decisions. They usually do not have plans for the days off. If the spouse asks them what they are going to do for the weekend, their response is: "well, I don't know. What do you want to do?" Their spouse always replies to them that she expected for them to select, plan and decide what to do. Their usual response is: "I am okay with whatever you want to do." And they end up going nowhere.

They want to stay home to "rest" and watch TV. They encourage the spouse to go grocery shopping while they wait at home. They do not have the desire or energy to play with or help their children with homework. They want for the spouse to make and execute all plans for the family. They drive the car under the spouse's directions. Most often, they occupy the passenger seat, the spouse controls the wheel while they pretend to be in charge. They play hard to get. They enjoy being BETAs.

It is not a bad thing to be a GAMA person, as long as the person is mature, centered, and has the intellectual ability to behave adequately at the appropriate time.

Nowadays, GAMAs are popping up everywhere because society so demands it.

ENERGY CALCULATOR:

Now you know more about the ALPHA, BETA, and GAMA energy. You are wondering which energy you have, I bet. Wonder no more! Why don't you find out? Below, you can find the ENERGY CALCULATOR. Once you answer your questions, you will find that you are not a 100% ALPHA, BETA, but don't worry about it; that is the way it is. It is natural. No one in the world, not even King Salomon or Alexander "The Great" were 100% ALPHAs. Every one of us has a combination of ALPHA and BETA energy. We are concerned about discovering which type of energy is more predominant within us and rules our behavioral actions, daily.

This calculator has been designed to calculate your energy based on the questions we asked and the answers we provide to it. It will show you what type of energy you currently possess based on the answers you provide. If your results show you are a 70% ALPHA, 30% BETA, don't sweat it. You discovered your predominant energy is ALPHA with tendencies of BETA and GAMA. Basically, you are more ALPHA than the others.

Now, let's say you are not happy with the results. Great! You can always change the results by altering the way you think and act. If you want to be more ALPHA, just think what change you will accept and, then, act on it with daily consistency. Consistently monitor the thoughts and actions you expect that will alter your energy results. An old habit is only replaced by a new habit. You need to identify which habit you want to eliminate and which new habit you will adopt. For instance, I replaced the evening couch with a 30 minute workout. One of my friends told me he smoked marijuana in the evenings because, according to him, he slept "like a baby" afterwards. I recommended for him to do the Insanity Work-out for just 30 minutes, then he will REALLY sleep like a baby. He is still wondering if it is even worth it for him to replace a short-term memory deterioration with developing an acute memory sensory. Go wonder?! Replacing a habit is a matter of priority.

Another friend suffered from depression because she did not have a job she enjoyed. I told her to find a job she REALLY liked, which she did, and now she is the happiest person on earth!

It takes 21 days for your body to get used to dealing with body and mental changes. "It requires a minimum of 21 days for an old mental image to dissolve and a new one to jell," according to a study completed and published by Dr. Maxwell Maltz in 1960, whose work influenced nearly every major "Self-Help" professional from Zig Ziglar, Brian Tracy, Tony Robbins, and many more. His book, Psycho-Cybernetic has sold 30 million copies and is still selling strong. I highly recommend it to everyone ready to transcend to another mental world.

So, what energy are you projecting onto others and acting on as you go about your daily life? Specially, what energy are you projecting to women as you attempt to find "The One?" One factor is for sure: A man should never project or act on BETA or GAMA energy fully. A little bit of BETA energy is fine. ALPHAs need to be able to express emotions and feelings (BETA energy) to his mother, spouse, children, and significant others, without disregarding his position as an ALPHA male. When you act, think as if your energy and attitude is what you want to project. What you project is what others perceive. People will deal with you as they perceive you, either ALPHA, BETA, or GAMA. As always, you have the last word on it. Only you can decide how others must treat you. Let's move on to our Energy Calculator.

This is how it works: Read the question carefully. THINK the question with serenity. Reminisce on past events and how you acted on them to make a decision. Answer the question with a 1 (for Yes) or a 0 (for No).

ENERGY CALCULATOR

Question	YES	NO
I expect others to follow my instructions		
I avoid arguments at any cost		
If I want something really bad, I will fight for it		
New experiences make me nervous		
I must satisfied my partner no matter what		
I must be directed to accomplish a goal		
My friends must always be happy with me		
I like for other to be the initiators		
I am very considerate about for other people's opinion		
If I am rejected by someone I like, I keep on trying until I win them over		
Crows of people make nervous		
When I screw up, I own my error		
Life is too short to take it serious		
Loneliness freak me out		
I like very violent games		
Life is a party and we should live that way		

I say what I think and feel		
I don't finish projects on time		
I don't have a schedule to control my time		
Creating goals and objectives is boring		
I see a world of limited resources		
I enjoy to prove people wrong publically		
I walk my talk		
Money is evil		
I worry when other people have problems		
Football players are too rough		
I get nervous when ask to make decisions		
I like people telling me what I want to hear		
Taking the lead is not my thing		
It is my way or no way		
I scream when I am under pressure		
I don't like people getting upset at me		
I love playing contact sports		
I am flexible with my final decisions		
I love chatting and consoling my friends		
I am always looking for the next challenge		

If the circumstances are not there, I make the circumstances		
I do not fight, I dialogue.		
I belief in the survival of the fetus		
If I want it done correctly, I have to do it myself		
It is okay to procrastinate or do not show to appointments		
I get upset if people do not pay attention to me		
If people do not tell me I am doing great, I stop doing what I am doing		
My business comes first, no matter what		
I let others take credit for my work to avoid confrontations		
I am my own motivator		
I am a very nurturing person		
I have an entrepreneurial spirit		
Blame others when things go wrong, take credit when things go right		
People must listen to my opinion		
I'm timid with people I don't know		

ALPHAs Are Not Controllers; They Are Leaders

Before we get started on this topic, let me state something: A man is supposed to be an ALPHA and behave like wise. A woman is supposed to be BETA and behave as such. A GAMA is a GAMA and behaves as such. I said before and I say it again: ALPHA, BETA, and GAMA energy can land on either gender. The predominant type of energy a person projects depends on the type of parenting we receive at home, the influence our friends exert on us, and how the media shapes and shape our thinking.

Men, it is your responsibility to learn how to become an ALPHA. Either, you learn how to become an ALPHA or live with the consequences of not being one, good or bad (most likely). To illustrate this essential point, I am going to get a little intimate with you. Let me tell you my personal, life-changing story. Ever since I can remember, I knew I was born a male. I grew up with the "rough-and-tough" males, fighting, soccer, wrestling, daring, etc. I still remember my Dad telling me I owe to protect, not mistreat, females. He would tell me "the male is the man of the house, the protector, the provider."

I entered the Mexican Army with that mentality regarding women. I was 15 years old. I spent months performing my military duties. I exchanged punches and bullets with the bad-boys. There was not a woman among us in my military post. So, I kept on growing up with male figures. On my days off, I would visit bars, dancing places, and get drunk while telling army stories to the girls at the bars. I would buy drinks and flowers for the girls as a reward for spending time with me. I wanted sex. They were there to serve that purpose. We both knew it.

I also developed romantic relationships with the more "decent" type of girls in town, family girls, you know. Again, flowers, dinners, movies, dancing, and spending money on them. After spending a week or two, I would hear from the girls no more. I invested my hard-earned money buying stuff for them. I wanted to impress them. That was my way to show them my attraction for them.

Way too many times women rejected me. Way too many times I had a bad case of blue balls. This constant rejection made me shy away from talking to women. I tried talking to women at malls, on the street, and at restaurants just to find a rain of rejections. So the girls at the unholy places and the girls at the socially acceptable places rejected me. I was not scoring with any woman. My self-esteem went from 10 to 0 in no time. Women rejected me so much I became intimidate by them. Afraid of them, you can say. So, I grew up into my adulthood afraid and intimidated by women. Even though, I was "rough-and-tough" with other men, I was wimpy with women.

There was this one time when a pretty woman took a look at me and gifted me her smiled. That smile got me really excited. Finally, somebody was paying attention to me. Somebody found some type of value in me, I thought. Somebody likes me and finds me attractive. I was happy! I talked to her timidly. I invited her out. She accepted my invitation. I was blown away. I couldn't believe it. I was a street warrior and wimpy with women. I couldn't reason how this invitation and acceptance had just happened to me. It was a happy day to say the least!

I dated this woman for about two months and then moved in with her a year later. This woman understood that I was at her disposal, at the snap of her fingers, from the get-go. Anything she requested, I acted on it rapidly. Washed dishes, cleaned up the house, picked her up at work, grocery shopping, car wash, laundry, you name it, and I did it. She went out with friends and would come home late. She would almost never cook, clean the house, do laundry, exercise, or anything that cause her to fulfill her responsibilities as the woman of the house. She lived at the malls and at her relatives' houses. I did not argue with her about it. I did not want to cause her pain. She was so special to me. I couldn't say no to her doing activities I did not agree with. I did not want to make her angry at me. I was just so happy she had accepted me. I did not want to be rejected and lose her. I was afraid I would end up solo, again. I consoled myself by saying, "you know, Alfredo, we are in America. New generation. New era. New way of doing things. Besides, she is with me". I made up excuses for her to justify her behavior and mine as well. I told myself that I needed to protect and take care of her.

If she did not feel like going to a special event, I did not argue and stayed home with her. She would change meaningful occasions for meaningless occasions and I was okay with that. She loved watching TV and I became accustomed to it, too. When she mentioned she was tired, I did not bother her. When she complained about work or life itself, I listened and supported her. I gave her the freedom to do whatever she needed to do. I did not want to be a problem, a pest, to her. During the process, I became accepting and complacent.

Even though I was experiencing a miserable life and lived with emotional pain for years due to daily frustrations, I still refused to leave her. I was uncertain about my future. I was confused. I lost sight and direction in my life. I did not have dreams any more. She was my focus of attention and I forgot about me. I believed we had something special, although we each lived in our own reality show. We lived in the same house with opposite directions in life. She called the shots for almost everything. I went along with her orders to make her happy. I played the "Good-Husband" role to not disappoint her. Gradually, we grew apart. She told me she needed her space. She slept in her room and I slept in mine. No sex whatsoever for months at a time. We lost the attraction and affection for each other, slowly. The relationship became sour and pitiful. Our relationship was beyond repair. Our relationship died. Actually, our relationship had died years before, I just refused to recognize and accept this fact for fear of her leaving me. We ended up going our own way, anyways. I ended up alone, again.

After too many rejections, again, I met another woman. She was from a different town. Different background and culture. More understanding. Very pretty and great body. We went out three times and we hooked up. We did not even have two months dating each other and I was already making plans to move in together. I envisioned her as the mother of my children, as a great mom, as a great wife, us having a wonderful life, and how beautiful things were going to be with her on my side. So what happened?

She figured me out within 3 months. She understood that I was a "good-husband" material: obedient, complacent, docile, and submissive. I asked her to be a stay-home wife and I will provide for us. She was happy about my proposition. Soon, she made it clear that she would not make me a morning cup of coffee, cook, do laundry, or house chores, even if her life depended on it. She slept 10-12 hours a day. Although, she could not keep her house neat and in order, she managed to always present a nice physical appearance. She was not too bright, but bright enough to know I liked her and needed her to be happy and by me. She made me feel valued and special. I had found someone to share my life with was my thinking. I resolved to do anything within my power to make things happen for her, so she would not leave me. She was more than ready to go along with my neediness and submission. I invested a lot of money on her. Anything you can think of, I gave her. She was in heaven. So here I was again, dealing with the situation of giving, buying affection, you can say, to be accepted. I have been rejected so many times; I was not willing to let this woman toss me away. She was just too pretty and owned a wonderful body! I was excited to have someone like that next to me. I was happy to eat all her bull-shit as long as she would not leave me. She was happy about her life style. I was happy she was with me. I did not know where to go. I had no dreams. I was killing myself at work and with house chores. But, I refused to let go. I couldn't do it. It was too painful. "Where am I going to find another woman like her", I would tell to myself. I felt sorry for myself and my situation. I was too weak to terminate the relationship. Our relationship ended regardless of my weaknesses and efforts. One day, she just did not come back home. She disappeared from my life, suddenly. I have not heard from her anymore. So, there I was, solo again! Another punch to my self-esteem, another failure! For my luck, I found another woman that would become a hurricane in my life. Let me tell you the story:

9

THE EVA CASE

I am going to share with you a very personal story. But before I tell you the story, let's keep something clear. I am sharing this story to back up a point or a concept. I am not sharing this story as a source of gossip or to solicit compassion from people, or to give other people a bad name. It is simply to back up the point or a concept I want to illustrate. Let's call this story: The Eva Case.

I am glad I experienced this relationship. It changed me for the better as a person, and on how I deal with women and business nowadays. It is what motivated me to complete an auto-analysis and to reinvent myself. I experienced too many relationship failures, but Eva was the main and final motivator that inspired me to write this book. I am grateful to her. She motivated me to become a strong ALPHA man.

I met a woman at one of my financial services seminars. I was the lecturer and trainer. She was an attendee. Let's call her Eva. A suitable name for her. Single Mom. Boyfriend on "the side." Living on her own. Low-end factory clerk worker. She was beautiful from head to toe. Silky, long and shiny black hair, friendly smile, sensual personality, enchanting and charismatic attitude, well sculptured face and body, very feminine. My dream girl.

She was a distraction in my seminar. She always seemed excited. She joined my company. I became her mentor. I persuaded her romantically. She was not bothered by it either. I over texted, emailed, and phoned her. She took control of my time and my emotions from the very beginning of our interaction. We became lovers. I moved into her apartment two months after meeting her. I felt grandiose and somewhat accomplished. I had my dream girl with me. She was as beautiful as a model.

As you can tell, I made a decision based on external beauty. I didn't take the time to verify if our values and principals were comparable. Her life style was the opposite of my life style. I did not care. I was willing to give it a shot. "I bet I can change her," I said to myself. "Once we start to hang around together, she will learn to be a classier woman with a superior life-style. I will teach her to be a business woman." I was sure I could mold her into my ideal woman, business and family oriented. Boy, did I pay a price for overlooking inner beauty.

I asked her for us to move together. She accepted. She walked away from her job upon my request. I did not want to chance losing her to another guy. I was a very successful financial advisor, I owned beautiful houses, I made lots of money, and I could take care of her. I did not want my future wife to be a garment factory worker in a beat up building located in the ghetto part of Los Angeles. I ordered her to walk out from her job. I picked her up outside her work and drove her over to her apartment. I drove through a maze of dirty alleys to get to her 2-story apartment. The apartment was located along a filthy and lonely alley in a bad area.

She invited me to enter into her apartment. The kitchen was semi-clean and in disarray. The dishes in the kitchen sink seemed to have been there for days, so did the oily pans on the stove burners. The living room smelled damp, perhaps because the carpet was too old with a fading color. The furniture had seen better days. There were piles of boxes and clothing in the closet under the stairs leading into the 2nd. Level. The broken, closet door rested against the closet wall, as if forgotten. I did not care about her life style. I was happy I was with her. We kissed, made up, and then she led me into her bedroom located on the 2nd. Level.

I eyed her children's bedroom on my way into the master bedroom. It looked terrible. Unmade beds. Graffiti-like writing and a large hole on the wall. Shoes scattered all over the floor. Dirty clothes throughout the floor. Low-quality furniture. The room was humid and projected an image of abandonment. I did not care about her life style. I was happy I was with her.

I peeked into the restroom as we made our way to the master bedroom. It screamed HELP!! A complete disarray and unkept. Dusty and lose hair on the floor, dirty mirror, hair in the sink, yellow stains at bottom and around toilet, trash container over filled with what seemed to be napkins and toilet paper, air-dryer, nail polish, make-up rested on the vanity sink. It was a sad bathroom. I did not care about her life style. I was happy I was with her. Besides, we were getting closer to her bedroom.

Finally, we made it into her bedroom. It was kept in the same way as the kitchen, the closet, the children's room, and the bathroom. She made up a mini-story to excuse herself for not making her bed before heading out to work, for the shoes and clothes that laid scattered on the stinky, dark brown carpet and under her bed, the over-filled closets which vomited old papers, boxes, and garments out of them. I validated her story. I was with her in her bedroom. Nothing else mattered. I did not care about her life style. I was happy I was with her. Finally, I had found "The One," I thought. "Once she is with me, she will change." What a first experience! Let me tell you about the second experience.

Our company invited me to vacation in Cabo San Lucas, Mexico, for a business retreat. I brought her over with me. All expenses paid by me. At the end of the first day, the guys attending this retreat desired to party at a local bar in town. You know, dancing, drinking, and fun! I did not care for it. I wanted to be with Eva. Our relationship was fresh. I wanted to know her more. Eva did not agree with me. She wanted to party with the guys, too. I told her I had other plans for us. She did not listen. She decided she wanted to have fun with the guys at the local bar. She dressed up, got totally ready, and walked away out of our room to the reception desk to meet up with everybody else. I stayed in the room. She disregarded my plans, my consent, my thinking, and my pleading to stay with me. A big-time blow on my self-esteem.

She returned to the room around 3 a.m., after hanging out with the guys. I was happy she was back and decided to spend the rest of the night with me. I was thankful. Whether or not something happened with her and someone else while she was out partying, she is the only one to know. I only know that those 8 hours of waiting for her drilled me slowly and painfully in my heart and my brain. Even though I was super pissed off with her, I was quick in justifying her behavior. I thought, "Well, she is a single mom. She probably hasn't had fun for a while. She is at a different place. She just wants to have fun. Besides, I had the opportunity to go with her. I chose not to." I manufactured and bought my own stories to justify her attitude. She noticed I wasn't upset upon her return. She was not in trouble. She also discovered I was a needy man. I eat up my anger and frustration to avoid confrontations with her. We finished our business trip and returned to the U.S.A, as if nothing had happened.

She took control of our relationship. I remember a time she left me waiting for her outside the Walmart for 3 hours. I fell asleep. She came back to the car, as if everything was normal. I told her it was not okay for her to leave me in the car waiting for her for so long. She smiled, raised her voice, and said to me that she was not in the mood to argue. She closed the door, ordered me to drive, and remained silent, with her eyes looking into the distance. I eat up my anger and frustration again.

Since she was a stay-home mother, her main responsibility was to attend her children, me, and the house. I forgot to ask her if she was okay with that! I discovered that she loved to over sleep. The children ran late for school most of the time. It was always the children's fault. Man, I don't remember more than 5 times in 7 years we were together that she sent the children to school with food in their stomach. It was an offense to her to ask her to make me a cup of coffee, and when she did, it was a bad coffee with bad company, if she did not go back to sleep. I accepted the situation because I didn't want to hurt her feelings by confronting her with something so special to me.

She loved shopping with her family and friends. Why make the beds, pick up the rooms, wash dishes, do laundry, clean the bathrooms, kitchen, prepare food consistently when time is on your side; keeping a house in order and neatly can always wait for tomorrow; and what a better way to spend time than by jumping from store to store and restaurant to restaurant with her family and friends. That was her way of thinking. She understood well that she knew how to control the situation if I were to confront her about her irresponsible habits. She just needed to raise her voice at me and I would become quiet. She knew I hated arguments with her. Of course, I did not agree with this shopping deal. But, it was better for me to keep quiet and give in to her way of thinking.

I remember those dinner night at the house. I can still picture her running from the street into the kitchen to prepare dinner, that is, if she had not eaten at some restaurant or had brought the so famous "Chinese Food." She was magical. She could prepare dinner within 30 minutes most of the time. Healthy and unhealthy food. She was a good cook, though. By 7 or 8 pm, dinner was ready. Almost no talk at the table. Picked up dishes after dinner and placed them at the sink to wash them whenever anyone felt like it; sometimes right away and other times the evening after.

There was no way I could win an argument with her. She knew it all. She knew every answer in the book and was never wrong. I could have written down a book on all the times she was wrong with her proof that she was right. The words "I am sorry and I apologize" were not part of her vocabulary. It was an offensive gesture for her to offer. I don't remember these words coming out of her mouth one time in 7 years. I might be wrong, but I just do not remember them.

Gradually, my life became the reality I always said I did not want for me or my family. I did not want to have a relationship based on drama. I never saw myself living a mediocre life style. I did not want to be any one's "doormat." And, yet, there I was, living that very life style. I lost all my houses and my money. I went from riches to misery in no time. From a great mental attitude to a mediocre attitude.

After losing millions of dollars in money and property, I ended up on the streets. No place to take my family to. It was then, when I discovered the value of 99 percent of friends and family. Once family and friends figure out you are broke, you quickly find out how much you really are worth to almost 100 percent of them.

One of my brothers offered me to stay in his house. One room, small room, for 5 people: Eva, her children and I. His house was decent and he offered to help me out with work while I find a new vision for my life. Eva refused my brother's help. She accepted her family's help, instead. I did not like the area where her parents lived nor their life-style, dirty, disarray, alcohol, fighting, child abuse, disrespect, etc. etc., you name it, it happened. I never saw myself and always ran away from living that life style. Nevertheless, I accepted to move in with them and adopted "my new way of living."

They had an empty studio at the back of their house. Naturally, I thought, they would allow us to occupy the studio. Why not? What parent would not help her child to get back on their feet? Cats and dogs occupied the studio at the time. Naturally, they defecated and urinated inside the studio. So the studio needed a complete clean-up and hygienic treatment. We had an 8 month old, baby-girl with us. Last thing I wanted is for the baby to catch a virus of some sort and put her in the hospital. Her parents did not offer for us to occupy the studio. Their offer was for us to sleep in the house living room, on 10 year-old sofa bed, next to a couple of Chihuahua dogs. Eva wanted to stay with her parents. I had to accept their proposition. I had just lost everything I owned and worked for, day and night, for over 15 years. I was living my mental burial alive. I did not have time to argue about these NEW living conditions. I just ate it up. I did not want to upset Eva.

To my bad luck, the same day I moved into Eva's parent's house, I became disabled. The sciatic nerve put me on my back for almost 2 months. What a pain. I was paralyzed for about one week. I laid down and rested my back on the dirty and cold tile floor for two weeks. Eva's parents expected for us to at least pay our own expenses and pitch-in a little with house expenses and chores. I did not have any savings and could not earn money due to my back problem. I felt useless. I cried in loneliness out of frustration and hopelessness. I asked Eva that if we would move over with my brother, we would not have to worry about money or food. Her children would attend quality schools. We would live in a clean home and nicer area. She disagree. I stayed quiet.

So, Eva, my baby-girl and I had to sleep for two months on an over 10-year old sofa bed in the living room, next to a pair of barking, Chihuahua dogs. The sofa bed was so old it showed the framing metal bars and my back could prove it. We went to sleep when the last person got tired of watching TV and woke up when the first person woke up.

The dogs' barking and crying and the smell of dogs' poop became ordinary every mid-night. Almost no intimacy. I hated it. Eva kept refusing to leave her parents. I became depressed.

Once I felt recovered mentally and physically, I visited my great friend, Dennis Shoenfelt, my adopted Dad, as I call him, and he gave me a job. Eva's parents found out I was about to start work and offered to rent out the studio to us. I couldn't believe it. They had their daughter (forget about me and the baby-girl) sleeping under deterrent conditions because she did not have money to pay them for the studio. I realized at that very moment, how much their daughter was worth to them. And to think that Eva forced me 2 years before to pay thousands of dollars for her Mother's trip to Hawaii with us. I hold no grudge against them nor do I regret paying for her trip. On the contrary, I am grateful to them for the priceless lesson they have shown me. I asked Eva for us to move away, she refused. I learned at that time that Eva did not deeply comprehended the value her parents placed on her and her happiness. I also verified the value she placed on me and her children. I nodded my head side to side and remained quiet, in deep thought.

I started a new handyman business soon after renting the studio. No more Financial Services or Real Estate. We moved into a 2 bedroom apartment 7 months later. We stayed 2 miles away from her parents. Eva wanted to stay close to her family. Same bad area. I improved my life financially, a little bit at a time. Then, I started to change my life for the better. Still, I couldn't have Eva move away from her parents so we could enhance our family life-style. I spoke up my disagreement about it. She did not like it. We separated. I walked away empty handed. My self-esteem was fully recovered, though. She kept the business and ran it down the gutter. It was expected.

I was determined to make money and move on with my life. So, I built another handyman business. The business gave me results promptly. Eva shows up 4 months after our separation. She convinces me to get back together. She promises she would become a better partner. She will even participate in the growth of the new business.

So we moved in back together. 6 months later, Eva asked if she could have access to the business finances completely. I noticed she was making improvements at home and at the business. She switched the business ownership from the original owner to her name. She opened bank accounts under her name. We leased a building under her name. We purchased work trucks and vans under her name. She transferred everything under her name. I thought she was trying to be an active participant in the business. She showed interest in learning a little bit about the financial part of the business. I saw it as a good sign. She could handle finances and I could handle operations, I said to myself. I was happy. Everything went well for about 11 months until the old Eva resurfaced, again.

Her old attitude reappeared. Waking up late, problems with children, avoiding house chores, late dinners, and lots of arguments. You name it, it happened! Then, she proposed to me, the ultimate in vulgarity. She told me I did not know how to be a strong man and did not know how to guide my family. For that reason, she connected with the pastor of her church. She knew the pastor for no more than two months. She volunteered our house for the pastor to visit and give instructions on the "Word" and how to live by the "Word". I did not agree with her or the pastor. She did not care, she did it anyway. I kept silent.

She requested for me to attend weekly sermons in our house on how to be a good man and husband and create good families. Don't get me wrong. I am a very spiritual man. I believe in the existence of something or someone greater than us. She continued with the sermons anyway. Sermons started every Monday at 6pm and would be over by 10 pm. I went to Starbucks instead to plan my next day business schedule. I did not want to confront her about these religious teachings. I let her do her thing. She became offended because I did not attend those sermons. I did not argue. I just wanted to get back home and sleep. Since the moment the pastor entered into her life, she backed up every argument with bible verses. She became a fanatic of organized religion. My children became fanatics of organized religion. My family now follows the leadership of another man. They refused to follow the leadership of the man that works for them and pays the bills for everything. I ate up my frustration and anger, again. I kept quiet.

Naturally, we started to have bigger problems. Heated arguments, insults, angriness, disappointments, etc. She followed her way of thinking and I followed mine. We had different expectations in life. It came to the point that she felt used by me. Things were just not happening for her. She blamed me for that. I tried to bring clarity into her thinking and she shut me down quickly. I did not say one more words because I was afraid to lose her and end up alone. Just like in the past.

So for keeping my mouth shut, I became complacent and her "doormat." Our relationship deteriorated. Our emotions and feelings faded away. I couldn't wait for the day to light up so I could go to work and hated the evening because I had to go back home. Even though my children were at the house, I had to go back home and face her. She drained my batteries. She made me feel ugly and disgusted about myself. Seeing her was about facing the reality of my life. I hated this feeling. I hated it very much.

For years I put up with this Bull-shit. But, I was not willing to walk away from my children. I kept hoping she will shape up. She would change. And change she did, she used to leave everything to me, now she leaves everything to God. "What about you giving God a hand to make things happen for you? He already has too many customers to serve," I told her many times. She thought I was making fun of her religion. She did not get my point. I left it at that. Eva complained to me one day that I was an unexciting, boring, and dull person.

Finally, and to my surprise, I made the decision to walk away from Eva and the place I disliked so much. I told her that I was moving away with or without her. I told her I had found a place where I want to take my family to reside. There are quality schools there. The life style I want is there. You and I can have a fresh start. She argued against it.

She decided to take a vacation out of the country. Upon her return, she showed up unexpectedly in our office. She called me into the office to inform me that she is closing down the company. I told her she cannot do that. This company was feeding her children, herself, and employed her family. Besides, I started this company. I owned the company and I told her so. "I worked day and night building this company. My efforts and this company paid for your recent vacations. It pays for your house, your clothes, your food, your gas, your parties, your friends and family expenses, it employs your family, 12 employees and their families depend on a check from this company to pay for their bills. You know this company is mine." "Not really," she told me. "Everything under this company is under my name. From the lease of the building to the truck your drive. Everything is mine. You are an employee of this company.

You work for me. Either I take full control of the company or I am shutting down the company." I told her to shut it down.

Right away, the receptionist called in all the employees. Eva told them the company is "shutting down." She also told them that she intended to continue with the operations of the company. She invited them to stay. Everybody walked away. They thanked her for the short notice. Eva looked at me and demanded for me to return the key to get into the building. The very person to whom I trusted with my family and my business, whom I feed, dressed up, and supported for years, chopped my head off. I refused to give her the keys. She called the police on me. The police arrived and demanded for me to evacuate my company. Eva talked to one of the two offices. The officer approached me and demanded the keys for my new truck. I surrendered the keys. Then, two police officers escorted me out of the building and released me on the building's parking lot. Eva smiled at me. I turned around and walked away. As I made my way toward my house, I thought: "Eva has, legally, stolen my company and destroyed my family, let alone 8 years of my life. How did that happen? WHY did I allow it to happen?!"

6 Months later, after seriously analyzing the reason for my separation, I realized I was the only one at fault. I didn't know how to be a man. "YOU ARE WEAK", she told me several times. She was correct. I tried to be a generous man and she saw me as a weak, needy man. She saw stupidity in

my humbleness. I did not put a stop to her perception and behavior. I can make this assessment now, because now I understand what it means to be a Man. The man I wish I would have been since the beginning of my life.

Again, I am sharing this story to back up a point or a concept. I am not sharing this story as a source of gossip, to solicit compassion, or to give other people a bad name. Simply to back up the point or a concept I am illustrating. So what is the point of my story: If you allow others to take over the reigns of your life, they will!

Let me ask you a question. Can you identify who I was? ALPHA, BETA, or GAMA? And what type of energy I projected? ALPHA, BETA, or GAMA? If you answered BETA or ALPHA you are partially correct. The correct answer is GAMA. I was a tiger on business and a pussy in my house. So how an ALPHA would have handled the Eva case?

First of all, an ALPHA would have made a decision if Eva was marriage material or sex material based on the conditions she kept her apartment. I can answer this question with clarity now. For me Eva should have been just sex material, friends with benefits, that's all. Making this decision would have saved me 7 years of penitence.

An ALPHA is the leader and commands respect. When Eva went to party with friends in Cabo San Lucas, he would have set her straight or simply end the relationship right then. Basically, let her be someone else's problem. I can see that she would have not been neither sex nor marriage material. I should have dropped her on the spot and forget about her.

See how easy it is to make decisions on challenging situations once you know the answer to the challenge. For this reason, it is imperative for a man to understand energies and how they are projected and represented. Once you identify energy through actions, you can select who is marriage material, a sex-buddy, or straight dump.

It is extremely important for a man to know how to be an ALPHA. Why is it important? It can help him determine who he is and stands for. Had I known how to be an ALPHA male, my life would have been much easier, much more centered? I would have handled every relationship differently. I would have carried myself totally the opposite way. My end result on every relationship would have been different, more favorable. My life would be richer and more joyful. I did not know how to become an ALPHA male. No one took the time to guide me through the ALPHA process. I was having a hard time trying to understand me. I did not want to invest time on understanding other people. Let alone thinking about becoming an ALPHA male, trying to understand me and investing resources in me, to better myself, bettering my thinking, and making sure that everything I say and do is congruent with my goals and visions in life was not a priority to me. I was more concerned in understanding other people and how I can make them happy. I disregarded *the fact that everything starts with me.* No wonder I ended up unhappy. Every person that has lived with an unhappy person will tell you that it is hell to live with sad people.

So, I needed to know and profoundly retain what it means to be an ALPHA male. See, by mastering the concept of ALPHAs, BETAs, and GAMAs changes your paradigm. It changes everything. It puts the game results in your favor. It changes you to start with. It puts you in control. It enhances your perspective in life. It strengthens you spiritually, emotionally, psychologically, and financially. It betters everything in your life. Everything!

So, I made it my purpose to re-invent myself. I did it with the commitment that never again would I allow anyone to bring drama and destruction into my life. My life will be clear and simple. I promised to myself to become an ALPHA male with the capacity to identify BETA and GAMA energy and handle them correctly.

10

RELATIONSHIPS:

ALPHA

BETA

GAMA

Let's talk about a relationship. In this context, a relationship occurs between two people: A male and a female. This is the natural, God-given relationship. Sure we also have same-sex relationships. The energies apply to homosexual relationships as well. So, I am going to acknowledge every relationship. The law of energies do not discriminate. They apply equally whether you are turned on by the opposite or same sex. What matters in the relationship is who is the ALPHA, BETA, and GAMA.

Let me ask you a questions. Who is the ALPHA, the BETA, or GAMA in your relationship?

Do you or does she project the energy according to who you are?

What actions do you need to project to be congruent with who you are?

We already know an ALPHA is an ALPHA here and there and everywhere. This energy is the leader, the strength, the protector in the relationship. BETA energy supports, follows, cherish, loves, and submits to the ALPHA energy. It is the fragile and tender energy an ALPHA must protect. It is the ALPHA's complement, if you will. GAMA energy is the variable energy; it is the ALPHA and the BETA combined. This energy changes depending on the occasion and the place. GAMA energy can be A BETA in the house and an ALPHA in the street or vice versa. Whichever the case, two energies come together to form a bond, a relationship between two people, disregarding sexual preference.

I visited a coffee shop inside a large mall. I purchased a cup of coffee (an Americano), took possession of a table and a chair that gave me maximum visibility to study people as they walked in front of me. Hundreds of people, of all ethnicities and social statuses, frequented this mall. I wanted to see how people behave when they don't realize or have a clue that somebody is watching and analyzing how they walk, talk, look, dress up, hair style, toe nails, jewelry, basically, how they behave publically, at its natural habitat. What I discovered hit me as hard as the punch Marquez applied to Pacquiao the night Marquez became the champion.

Men, nowadays, seem afraid to claim, publically, what rightfully belongs to them. They seem uncomfortable with the idea of offering confidence and leadership to a woman. They have become lazy or complacent in the relationship. Too many of them are very comfortable with expressing a more feminine, BETA, energy

I saw over a hundred couples passing in front of me at the coffee shop. 95% of these couples walking around the mall behaved as if they were at the mall by themselves. The men and the women wandered around the corridors in different directions, they seemed as if they were lost in the mall. The woman 10 feet behind her man, as if following by force o simply being at the mall on her own, or vice versa.

Some couples seemed disoriented, as if they did not know what they were there for, as if they have landed on the wrong side of the planet. No conversation. No hand-holding. No playful walking. No hugging. No kissing. No joking around. They looked bored. Unhappy just killing time before retiring to sleep.

Women, especially young women, have developed a more ALPHA energy. Men, especially young men, have developed a more BETA energy. What happened? Why did we surrender our natural energies and behave in the opposite way as we ought to behave? Well, meet the best couple below:

THE BEST COUPLE: LAZY AND POLARITY

Let me introduce you to two extremely important concepts. These two concepts together are the number one factor contributing to over 60% of separations and divorces in the world. One is Lazy and the other one is Polarity. These two concepts follow a process. Laziness is the beginning and Polarity follows it automatically. Lazy is what is sounds like and you and I understand: A person is unwilling to work or use energy. You are not willing to do anything for you or for anyone. You want to be left alone and not be bothered.

Polarity is an extremely powerful concept in a relationship. It is a life changing concept capable of making your life awesome or ruin everything around you. Polarity is "a state in which ideas or opinions, etc. are completely opposite or very different from each other", according to the Webster Dictionary. Basically, two energies coming together and acting out differently from how they should act. For example, you claim to be an ALPHA and you act with BETA energy, then you are entering into a state of Polarity. Your wife has a BETA energy and expect for you to have an ALPHA energy. So that means she is willing to place her trust and confidence in you. She expects from you to be the leader and the protector. The very moment you stop leading and protecting her, you relationship has become Polarized. Once you start to project a BETA energy knowing that you have projected ALPHA energy before, at that moment, you turned on the button of Polarity.

Let me illustrate with a personal example. I remember the Saturday morning when my girlfriend would ask me, "What are we doing this weekend?" (BETA energy), and I would give her my usual reply, "I don't know. What do you want to do this weekend?" (BETA energy). She would answer, "I don't know. Do you want to do something for the weekend? (BETA energy), she would press on. I would forcefully reply, "Let's do whatever you want to do" (BETA energy). We ended up going to places neither her nor I enjoyed.

What was she telling me in reality? You know, the hidden message. Let's run the scenario from her request along with the hidden message.

She said: "What are we doing this weekend, honey?" What she is really saying is this: Hey! You are the leader. In what direction are you leading us this weekends? Tell me the plans so I can follow you.

I said, "I don't know. What would you like to do this weekend?" What she heard is this: "Oops! I didn't think about us or anything for us to do over the weekend. I am blanking out. I don't know what to do or answer. I am confused. Help me. You be the leader. You guide us. I will be the female energy. Make a decision for us. Please".

She said: "I don't know, either. Come on! We got to do something?" What she really said is this: "Make up your mind, man! Make a decision already! Come up with something! You are supposed to be the leader here. How Am I supposed to follow you without a goal or a plan?"

I said: "We'll do whatever you want to do" What she heard was this: "Can you be the ALPHA, the leader? I don't want to take responsibility. I am too lazy to have a goal and a plan or to even think. Let me follow your goal and your plan, please. I really do not want to invest any type of energy on being the leader and taking us somewhere."

I became an ALPHA acting on BETA energy. She counted on me to lead the march for the weekend. I did not want to invest energy into planning the weekend activities for both of us. It was easier for me to pass my ALPHA responsibilities to her.

Had I known what I know now, my responses to her would have been different. When she asked me what we were going to do for the weekend, I would respond today with a "well, baby, for Saturday, Let's wake up late and have at breakfast home. Let's get our chores out of the way first because we are going out around 6:00 pm. It will be a formal evening so wear high-heels with a nice dress. We will be back late. Sunday, let's exercise early in the morning while the breeze is still fresh. We are having breakfast out of the house. I have a place in mind to have breakfast in, unless you have a specific restaurant you want to try out. We will be walking around the city all day long. So, wear something casual. We are coming back to the house around 6pm. Once we are back home, we will see what happens next" (ALPHA energy). An ALPHA leads.

See how easy it is to nail questions correctly when you know the answer to the questions!! The majority of women want to get in the car, sit in the passenger seat, and ride. Women expect for the ALPHA, the driver, to drive the car and KNOW where he is going. They do not mind driving the car EVERY NOW AND THEN and go where they want to go. If she drives the car 100% of the time, she will gradually get tired of it. She will find herself doing ALPHA activities. She will become uncomfortable with this. By now, you know, Polarity will penetrate your relationship. When this happens, ALPHA, you are in trouble.

There are times when a woman prefers to visit other places. She is not saying she does not want to go to the places you propose. She is simply saying that she would like to satisfy a curiosity she might have about a certain place and is telling you, by soliciting your support on it. The ALPHA still has to make the decision on her proposition. Let's say she says: "can we go to a different place?" You should say: "what do you have in mind?" She might say "well, I was thinking about visiting my family?" You as the ALPHA should welcome the invitation and say "well, let me think about it. I will give you my opinion in a few minutes". Then you wonder and consider which function will create the most fun for both of you. Once you decide, you give her your opinion: "honey, we will visit your family. We will have the most fun there. Good idea".

Now, if you don't agree with visiting her family, say so. Share the reasons why you don't support her idea of visiting her family. If you really do not like her family. You will have to communicate to her the reasons why you don't want to visit her family. Do it maturely, quietly, and peacefully when both of you are alone. Now if you like her family, you can simply say something like this: "Let's visit you family next week. I want this weekend to be just for you and me". Bottom line is this: ALPHA, *you have to make the last decision.* You are the leader. You guide. You determine if the path and goal is safe, correct, and enjoyable for both of you. Again: FOR BOTH OF YOU. Some people try to make other people happy while becoming miserable themselves in the process. Don't become miserable just to satisfy and make the other person happy. Women do not like this. This is BETA energy. This behavior will lead your relationship to Polarity. Then, you will be in trouble. Stand up for your opinions and beliefs! Women love men willing to stand up for what they believe is right.

Why is Laziness and Polarization so powerful? Let me tell you a story. After this story, you will understand why it is so powerful and vital to comprehend and catch yourself when you are becoming lazy and heading straight into Polarization.

You walk on a public place. You identify a pretty woman you really like. You see her. You start to think about the best way to approach and contact her. Should you just walk towards her and compliment her nails, her hair, or should you tell her how pretty she is, etc. You enter into this revolution of investing energy and time to find a way to approach and contact her. Finally, you gather the will and courage to approach and contact her. You invite her out. She accepts. Both of you agree to meet at a certain location. Both of you are now ready to invest time and energy. Both of you are excited about this new odyssey.

You both meet at a restaurant. You listen to her. Ask her questions to identify if this relationship is worth pursuing. Now you are investing energy, time and money. So you talk, have dinner, you pay the bill, and then, you both depart back to each ones house. You both start the text messaging and phone calling ritual. You both set up another date. This time you tell her you will pick her up at her house. You are a gentleman. Neatly groomed and great hygiene. The right cologne. Your car is clean and smells good. You select a spectacular restaurant for the evening. You pick her up. You notice she also went through the same ritual you went through, for the occasion. After dinner, you drive her back to her place. You wish for her to invite you inside her place. She doesn't. You are not too happy about it. You put up with it and drive back home.

You set another date. You both follow the same ritual as before. You pick her up. Dinner. Questions. After dinner and questions, you start to develop sentimental feelings for her, and so does she for you. As you drive her over to her place, you fantasize on her allowing you to enter into her place. You seduce her. You picture yourself kissing her. Touching her. Undressing her. Fucking her brains out. Nothing happens. You don't become disappointed or lose faith. You know it is a matter of time for both of you to have sex with each other.

After becoming sexually active with each other, both agree to become exclusive. You are willing to take the relationship to the next level. You date for some time and move in together. You both have invested plenty of energy, time, and money into your relationship. Finally, you get her and she gets you. You reach your goal and so does she.

You both are living together now. You reach your goal and you have the trophy and so does she. The challenges of getting ready to pick her up and picking her up are there no more. You figure, I already have the trophy in my house. She is with me. I don't have to chase her with text messages, phone calls, special dates, no more driving, no more selecting places to take her to, etc. I don't have to be neatly groomed any more. No more Friday night dancing, movies, walk on the beach. Why? She is with me already. Friday nights become a "honey, I am home. What's to eat? Let's watch a movie. Let's eat popcorn. Let's just stay home. I will do it tomorrow. Less kissing and hugging. Less desire for each other. Less fun. Little by little, we become lazy.

Your woman gradually starts to realize that she is doing the responsibilities of an ALPHA. She slowly discovers she can no longer count on her ALPHA to produce ALPHA results. She starts to act and project ALPHA energy. She takes her own self to fun places. She develops her own ways to have fun on her own. She notices her ALPHA no longer mows the lawn, takes the trash out, cleans her car, brings the bacon home, takes her to fun places, etc. She knows she cannot count on him. If she wants anything done, she will have to do it herself. She starts to act more ALPHA and starts to ignore her man. She develops and projects ALPHA energy. *The moment a woman starts to perform the tasks and responsibilities of the ALPHA male, at that very moment, she develops Polarity.* She starts to create and grow the idea of "why do I need this man in my life. When we are walking on the street he does not hold my hand, kisses me, or hugs me. He is not dirty with me. He is not nutty. He is lazy at home. Gradually, she starts to lose **appreciation and respect** for her man.

If the man asks her to cook something for him, she tells him to cook it himself. If he asks her to go to the movies, she tells him she is not in the mood, she will wait for him at the house. If he wants sex, she tells him she doesn't feel like it at the time. She starts to lie. If her man is not willing to do much for her, why should she be motivated to do any different? She understands her man is not a person she can look up to and make her feel proud of something. At that moment she says, you know what, I don't want to be in this relationship anymore. He is in his own world. I am in my own world. I am happy without trying to make other people happy. I will survive with or without him. She is contemplating separation. She sells herself on the idea that it is better for him to follow his path and for her to follow hers. The burning desire for each other is close to non-existent. The romance is not there anymore. Respect and appreciation is not as strong as before.

When she goes to the supermarket, she sees that other men still find her attractive and keep an eye on her. She discovers that the attention she needs to receive at home, she is receiving it from men on the streets. Now she has been teased by other men. She is now curious about other men. At any time, she will become vulnerable and needy. She will look for someone capable of making her feel like a woman again, alive. Somebody to talk to and can listen to her. Someone to play with. As we now know, when the student is ready, the teacher will appear. In other words, when she becomes needy and vulnerable, she will look for a man herself. She will initiate a new relationship: cheating. Naturally and eventually, a separation follows.

"Men!" you are responsible for identifying the moment you are becoming lazy. You are responsible for keeping the light on! It is your responsibility to assure the courtship continues permanently. Romance continues to infinity. The moment you stop courtship and romance with your woman, you are allowing for the lazy and Polarity factors to kick in. Once those two factors kick in, you will be as dead as a hamburger patty. You and your relationship are done!

12

THE MOMENT

OF

TRUTH

12

THE MOMENT

OF

TRUTH

I am about to share a life-changing moment with you. It has changed the life of many people who dared to explore their thinking and adjust their ideas according to their desires to become the person they wanted to be and create the life style they want to own. Just like them, you will have to challenge yourself and make your own decisions on your personal downfalls and expectations. The personal discovery and change is your personal responsibility. The only one capable of creating change in your life is YOU. If YOU want to, it will happen. Let me ask YOU this:

1. Who are you?
2. What energy do you project? ALPHA, BETA, GAMA?
3. Do you live your life according to who you want to be and project the energy you want others to perceive?

DO NOT CONTINUE READING ANY FURTHER UNTIL YOU ANWER THESE QUESTIONS.

I asked these questions to myself. I answered them by saying: I am male. I project GAMA energy. I do not live according to who I want to be nor do I project the energy I want to project.

A life changing discovery. I had finally found the reason to my relationship and business failures. I removed the cover off my eyes. Suddenly, everything became clearer. I felt at ease. I felt peace. I felt in control. I discovered who I was and whom I will be from that moment forward. I felt grandiose! I was, finally, liberated!

I bet you have invested time in studying the life of other people. I know I did. I read biographies, magazines, documentaries about celebrities, women and friends I wanted to know more about, etc. I know I am not alone on this one. So, if you are willing to invest energy, time, and money on the life of other people, which you probably will never meet and cause little or no impact on your life, why not invest this energy, time, and money on you. You deserve it! You are worth it! You will see yourself in the mirror daily. You live with you and your ideas daily. You can cause an impact in your life daily. You are the recipient of your consequences daily. So why not invest in you to become a better you? Only the people that do not believe they are worth the shot, will not invest in themselves. You decide if you are a worthy investment. It is your choice. It is your life. By the way, ALPHAs are ALWAYS worth the shot. They always look for way, means, processes, ideas, concepts that make them better personally and in business.

This is your time. This is your moment. A renewed YOU is awaiting to be unearthed. A new way of life lies ahead of you. Find a quiet place. No interruptions. You need to be left alone with your spirit, your emotions, your mind, and yourself. Analyze your past, your present, and your future life. Then ask yourself the four questions we talked about above. Answer them honestly. The truth starts with your own self! You deserve to know the truth. Invest the energy, time, and money understanding and reformulating YOU.

Experience and live your discovery and transformation, your reinvention, your personal reengineering!

If you are not willing to invest the energy, time, and money to reinvent YOU by answering these profound and thought-provoking questions, then it makes no sense for you to continue with this journey. The bus stops here for you. You need to get off of it. Don't waste your time reading any further. You are already where you deserve to be; Good or bad. If you have invested the time, energy, and money to answer your questions and you are fully satisfied with your answers, then, stay on the bus. You and I need to move on with our journey.

Already in a relationship?

If you are in a relationship with somebody, you should know who you are and what energy you are bringing into the relationship. Equally important, what is she bringing to the table. Understand HER with clarity. You, as the ALPHA male in the relationship, must, undoubtedly, know who you are and what energy you are bringing into the relationship and on what energy you are acting on. Just as important, you MUST understand what energy she is bringing into the relationship and on what energy she is acting on. It is imperative you grasp this method fully by now. I am about to introduce you to a process to help you identify the right person for you and weed out the rest. If you do not comprehend, right now, who do you want to be and the energy you want to project, STOP reading. Go back and solidify, with clarity of mind and willful acceptance, who do you want to be and what energy you will project to others and your expectations from others.

If you are an ALPHA and you are with or want to attract another ALPHA, so be it; as long as this is what you truthfully want from her. If you are an ALPHA and you are with or want to attract a BETA, so let it be; as long as this is what you truthfully desire from her. And the same is true if you are with or want to attract a GAMA. If you already have a GAMA in your relationship, fabulous! Congratulations! Whichever energy complements your energy is what matters the most here.

How to Decipher a Person?

How do I identify ALPHAs, BETAs, and GAMAs? Listen to what they say verbally and non-verbally. Words, expressions, and mannerisms they use to communicate their ideas and opinions. Are they aggressive or passive words, expressions, and mannerisms? Words, expressions, and mannerism will give you the **exterior** picture you need to decipher the energy a person wants to project to others. People, in general, will use, especially at the beginning of a relationship, words, expressions, and mannerisms leading into formulating and presenting an image you are comfortable with, accept, and buy. Justly, this method lasts only until the actions of a person make their appearance privately or publically.

The most powerful tool to decipher who a person REALLY is and the REAL energy she possesses is based on her ACTIONS. She can tell you she does not like chocolate just because she heard you saying you dislike chocolate. Later on, you see her buying a box of chocolate. She eats the entire box of chocolates at once. Then, you realize she was untruthful. Her words, expressions, and mannerisms were not congruent with her actions. Point of the story? Listen to what people say and then compare what they say to what they do. You want to know if a person is a good person. Hear what they say and observe how they treat other people.

Want to know if you are with or want to be with an ALPHA, BETA or GAMA energy? Listen to what they say and watch their actions. An ALPHA is congruent and consistent. He does what he says he will do. A BETA is incongruent and inconsistent. She says something and does something else. A GAMA speaks vaguely and their actions are unpredictable. They avoid giving their opinion and you never know how they will act, ALPHA or BETA. Now you know how to reveal the true person and the energy they project to others. Take a little bit on what they say and everything on what they do and you got them!

13

YOU ARE THE TROPHY

Why should any woman compete for you? What do you offer? Or better yet, do YOU even know what you offer and represent to others? To be the trophy, you need to become a person of value and meaning, someone family and friends admire and respect because you represent someone of value; mature women love this. You need to become the coveted trophy women are looking and willing to work for. When you are worth the shot, when you are really worth it, you don't chase women, you don't have to! They come by themselves!

For you to become coveted, you need to know your inner and outer qualities. The outer beauty is important, but the inner beauty is more important. Now, if you have both beauties, well... LUCKY... you! Your inner beauty includes your psychology, your spirituality, mannerism, and your emotions. Outer beauty has to do with your outer persona. Your body figure, your clothing, and grooming. Since we already talked about these beauties, I won't touch them again. However, you can read more about them on the section titled Relationships 101. Do not allow for people to determine for you how much you are worth. You decide by yourself how much you are worth. Only you know what you represent as a person, the beauties or values you possess, and the factors you can contribute to others. If, by now, you do not know this information about you, I will share with you the following The Discovery Table. It helped me identify with clarity and seize my own qualities. I am sure I will help you, too.

Top 10 Beauties I Offer: inner and outer Beauties.

This Discovery Table will help you put in perspective the reasons why you are a great catch, a coveted trophy. Be honest with your own self. YOU ARE AN ALPHA. Why should anyone pay attention to you and to the qualities you would bring into their lives? Fill in the table.

Process to fill in the table:

1. Fill in the table with the top 10 Beauties you offer by priority of importance

2. Select the top 5 Beauties out of the 10 Beauties by priority importance

3. Select the top 3 Beauties a person MUST have, and you are not willing to live without, out of the 5 Beauties you selected before by priority of importance.

MY DISCOVERY TABLE

PRIORITY OF IMPORTANCE = 1, 2, 3, 4, etc...

Priority	Inner Beauties	Priority	Outer Beauties

Now you know the beauties you offer to others. Your value. You understand what you bring to the table. How you can affect their lives. Live accordingly. Live your truth by your beauties. Integrity and discipline will be your best allies. Under any circumstances, don't say or promise anything to anyone you do not intend to accomplish or is not part of you. It is fun to see and experience your own personal growth and living daily as the person YOU want to become.

WHAT DO I EXPECT FROM HER?

By now, you must know and have accepted your inner and outer beauties. You know who you are and what you represent. You are ready to rightfully demand expectations from women. This Discovery Table is about her: Your Dream Girl. Let's use the discovery table below to build up your ideal, fantasy woman. How do you expect her outer beauty to be? Tall, dark, fit, etc. What about her inner beauty? Spiritual, romantic, outgoing, etc. Once you have completed the table, surf the internet and find a picture of the woman that comes close to your Dream Girl. See that picture daily. She needs to be present in your mind. Out of sight, out of mind. So when you see some looking like her on the streets, you can recognize her. It is powerful. Fill in the blanks just as you did for your own Discovery Table.

Process to fill in the table:

1. Fill in the table with the top 10 Beauties she must have

2. Select the top 5 Beauties out of the 10 Beauties by priority of importance

3. Select the top 3 Beauties a person MUST have, and you are not willing to live without, out of the 5 Beauties you selected before by priority of importance

HER DISCOVERY TABLE

PRIORITY OF IMPORTANCE = 1, 2, 3, 4, etc...

Priority	Inner Beauties	Priority	Outer Beauties

DON'T COMPROMISE YOUR INTEGRITY

Now you know what you offer to women and what you expect from women. Don't compromise your integrity, your character, or your expectations from a woman. Don't compromise just to fit in, be liked, or to be accepted. There will be a lot of people and opportunities that will challenge the integrity of your inner and outer beauties. You will be tested and tempted to betray who you are and what you expect from a woman.

The very time a woman does not offer or quits providing what you expect from her, that very time deserves a mature heart-to-heart talk with her, or an immediate relationship termination. If you and your expectation are not honored, you must be willing to walk away, to let go! However, if she delivers your expectations, you have to acknowledge her participation and actions. Stay on course. Stay centered and serene.

Immediate gratifications will be the biggest teaser and your greatest misfortune. Drugs and alcohol, when consumed obsessively, as well as illegal activities, have proven to offer dream and life destruction consequences; and not just for the person doing it, but often times for the people around the person doing it as well. ALPHAs are "the biggest man" of the picture. They live and stay above negative influences and weed out of their life toxic people; even if that means, walking away from their family. They are men of substance. Men of character. And so, should you be.

Experience your own evolution, from being just one more guy in the crowd, into a savvy, solid, admirable, integral, and respected ALPHA male. Live the results of being an ALPHA. When you walk among less accomplished people, they will sense and acknowledge your presence. ALPHA males do not need to brag about or step on a person's shoulders to project greatness and essence when are present; they just do. A lot of people will be intimidated by it. Do not feel uncomfortable. It is natural. It is rare to come across ALPHA males nowadays. So, it is normal for you and them to feel uncomfortable: You are a new man. A man of value and meaning. A man of purpose. Do not succumb to anyone or anything. Stay firm and confident. It is YOU... re-invented. Your God-given right.

TREAT EVERY WOMAN THE SAME

Every woman is the same, their ideas make them different. For this reason, you need to treat every woman in the same way. They are human beings and you must never forget this fact. So treat them as human beings. Don't make saints, virgins, and idols out of any one of them. Do not place any woman on a pedestal. The moment you give special privileges to a woman, you open the door for a woman to take control of your life. You will become submissive and needy. Women love ALPHA males not BETAS or GAMAS. Be fair to them publically and privately. If you see a mind-blowing, great looking woman, go ahead and say hello to her. On the same token, if you see a woman that is less attractive, go ahead and say hello to her as well. You are an ALPHA male. ALPHAs are centered people and wise. They love all colors and nationalities. Women will love you for your thoughtfulness. No woman likes to be perceived of a lesser value. A man that loves women is loved by women in return. It is this simple.

You already have created your model woman. Be patient. She will show up. What is out of this world is that she will come as you are becoming an ALPHA. You attract what you think about. It is a divine, unwritten law. Heavenly father will place her in front of you. And now you have the inner and outer beauties to identify her. Your fantasy woman will become a reality. Maybe she will not be 100 percent what you expect, but it will be closer had you not had your list of expectations for her.

FROM CHURCH:

I remember attending a wedding church ceremony. Two of my good friends, Silao and Britney, were getting married that evening.

The father asked them both: "Silao, do you promise to make this woman happy? Britney, do you promise to make Silào Happy?"

They both replied with an enthusiastically "YES".

Suddenly, I heard Silao's mother whispering to another lady sitting next to her, "How is Silao planning to make that woman happy if he cannot make his own self happy?"

Britney's mother, sitting behind us, interjected, "You know, I was thinking the same thing about Britney. How is she going to make Silao happy when she is 24/7/365 unhappy with herself?

2 Years later, Silao and Britney divorced. I asked them both about the reason for their divorce. Both spitted

out the same answer: "He/she could not make me happy." That was a valuable lesson to me. Do not enter into a relationship with the expectation that the other person will and has the responsibility to "make me happy." About 60 percent of divorcees promised themselves to make each other happy.

You cannot make a person happy and no person can make you happy. Only YOU can make your own self happy. It is your own responsibility to make sure you make your own self happy. You must be happy with or without companionships. If she is with you, you should be happy and if she is not with you, you should continue being happy. *You must be the source of your own happiness.* Once you are happy with your own self, with or without your companionship, then you can *share your happiness* with others and vice versa. You have reached individual maturity. Ready for the next level. RELATIONSHIPS.

14

LIFE

OF

A

RELATIONSHIP

The Line between the Numbers.

Everything has a beginning, a process, and an end. Relationships are not the exceptions. They have a start, a middle, and a finish. I call the middle: "The Line between the Numbers: X-----X." Started on and ended by. It does not matter that you know when the relationship starts or ends. What matters the most is what you accomplished IN BETWEEN -during the line and the process- not the beginning nor the end, that in "in between" would be the part which represents the relationship quality. The line represents the story of your relationship: your story, and the memories you will share with each other, your children, future generations, and with others as you age. This line will tell others WHO you both really were. The choice is yours. Know how to pick right from the beginning.

1. **Are You Happy With Yourself?**

   You need to be happy with yourself before you start dating women. An unhappy person is neither enjoyable nor appealing. *Be happy with YOU first,* with or without a woman at your side. You develop happiness when you do what you like and love. Loving yourself = your work, your life style, your beliefs, your hobbies, anything and everything that makes up your life. You ONLY do what you like and love, nothing else. Don't do what you hate as you will become vain and bitter and so will your life. No matter how good it seems. No one, especially a woman, would have a pleasant time with a rancid, complaining, angry man. In fact, these type of people should not even be part of your life because eventually and unconsciously, they will win you over to their way of thinking. Their philosophy is toxic and their outer beauty is unfriendly. Get rid of them, pronto!

When you enjoy everything you do, you have reached the point of individual maturity, your purpose, and success. A person is successful if he is deliberately doing what he wishes and wants to do, even if there are fewer economical rewards. If you like cooking, be a chef and watch how you will become really good at it. If you are a cashier at a grocery store and you are there because YOU want to be there, be the best cashier and do it with gusto; then watch how many people would want to ring their groceries with you. This is easy. Of course, financial rewards will follow, because it is a well-known, unwritten law: Superior performance deserves superior rewards. Superiority starts with your determination and acceptance to be the sole source of your own happiness. Now you are ready to meet women.

2. **Selection (lots of flowers to pick from)**

Treat all women the same. Remember the "make me happy story" I told a while ago? The same story applies here. Don't hold other people responsible for your own personal happiness because you will be disappointed with the results. Happiness is personal choice. It is YOUR responsibility (We talked about that already). Don't go around town looking for "<u>THE ONE</u> that will make me happy." True, there are plenty of flowers in the garden, but they should not be responsible for your emotions. *You are looking for the "The One that is happy with herself and complements your energy, chemistry, and expectations."* Don't chase them, let them come to you. Only a BETA energy chases women. "The One" woman who is right will show up without being chased.

There are many women in the world, and they come in all colors and cultures. Men have an ample selection to pick from. *Treat all women the same.* The majority of women you meet will not "click" with you and some may even ignore you, but that is to be expected, the energy and chemistry may simply not be there. For this reason, you need to talk to every woman. Don't place them in a pedestal. But see them all at eye level.

Approaching and talking to women provides for you a compatibility test. Are we good for each other? Do we feel comfortable with each other? During this process, if they appear to rebuff you or seem disinterested, don't take it personal, you don't know her well enough to understand why things don't click immediately. Simply, your energies and hers collided for the moment. She did not necessarily reject you. You may have just discovered that she may not be "The One." So, move on with your life. Talk to another woman, and another one, and another one, etc.

NEVER CHASE WOMEN and, specially, those who have rejected you. Chasing women is a BETA attitude, a feminine energy. Only needy and starving men chase women. Unlearned men, incapable of assimilating self-worth and the value they bring to others chase women. If YOU KNOW you are the trophy, you don't need to chase. If you chase, it may be because you, perhaps, feel a high sense of worthlessness. For this reason, you chase, beg, and cry in hopes that someone will feel compassion for you and give you some sense of worthiness and acceptance. Men, listen, there are plenty of women in your area. Next...

LET WOMEN COME TO YOU. By this statement, I am not advocating for you to become motionless and wait for the ladies to make the first move. You have to make the first move. It must be natural and unintentional. For you to attract women, women must equate you with fun. Basically, YOU = Fun. I have not met one person that has refused an opportunity to have lots of fun. It would be too stupid for someone to say, "You know, I do not want to hang around him. He is too funny, too hilarious, and too much fun! I would rather go out with the boring guy." You get the point, right? **YOU** MUST = FUN! Women must know that being with you is enjoyable, and then watch how you become a women magnet.

Women are attracted to happiness, fun and laughter. Either you are or must become the person that can offer these "goodies" to women. If you are funny, fun, and can make a woman laugh and give her a good time, congratulations, you are already there. If you are not, you will have to make the decision to become this person. The choice is yours. You can change if you want to. Read jokes. Attend comedy shows or funny movies, anything that makes you laugh loudly enough that it will bring tears to your eyes. Watch how you will start to share jokes, use funny phrases, even act a little goofy and women will smile more at you. And don't you care what they think about you? You are having fun, remember?

Now, if you do not want to become a fun person, no problem. You can be whatever you want to be. Just as there are boring men in the world, there are boring women as well. They are looking for their complement as well. They both are looking for a partner just like them. Your partner is somewhere among them.

Live a life of perpetual happiness. Everywhere you go, keep a smile on your face and gaze toward the distance, walking confidently. Project an image of self-control and peacefulness. The world is filled with men and women, so everywhere you go, say "hello" to the people making eye contact with you. Project happiness everywhere you go, work, coffee shops, movies, karaoke bars, restaurants, malls, parties, family gathering, grocery stores, and heck, even at funerals. Funerals, I said? Sure, you cannot say you are happy about death. But you can say you are happy for the gift of life. It all depends on how you communicate your message. Additionally, don't fake happiness. Be a happy person for real, and express happiness naturally. Be genuine! Since you are doing everything you want to do, expressing happiness should not be a problem for you anymore.

Don't go out with the idea or the objective to meet women. Go out with the idea of having fun. You are going to treat yourself, doing something you like. If you are going to the movies to watch a comedy presentation, laugh loudly and enjoy it. Even if people turn around to see you, ignore them, and keep on enjoying yourself. You are going to a bar to have fun not to specifically meet girls. No, you are there SPECIFICALLY to have fun! You attend a concert to listen to the performers, not solely to meet women.

Private parties are to mingle, not to specifically meet women. You get the point? Erase from your mind that you are going out for the sole purpose of meeting women. Going out for the sole purpose of meeting women is a needy, BETA, behavior, as if you are chasing women. If you are not planning to have fun, do not go anywhere. Save face. Adopt this new way of living, a new attitude that says "I am going out to have fun."

I still remember when I made the decision to adopt my new "I am going to have fun attitude." I met up with some friends at a restaurant. We were loudly sharing comical anecdotes, jokes, and just having pure fun. I noticed women would make it a point to pass by our table. They smiled at us. We smiled back and kept on goofing around. One woman stopped completely next to our table, looked at me, and said to us, "Somebody around here is having too much fun, I see. This must be the fun section." We replied, "It must be! These guys here are way too funny," I said. "They almost make me pee on myself." She smiled and went back to her table. We kept on having fun. Ten minutes later, she made her way to the restroom and stopped again on her way back to her table. We quickly looked at her and kept on goofing around. She stood next to me for a good minute. Then, she said to me, "I got to go back to the boring table over there," and walked away. I gave her a military salute with my right hand, blinked my right eye at her, and kept on having fun.

She came back to our table ten minutes later to say good-bye to us. Apparently she was leaving the bar with her friends. She asked me for directions to a popular dancing bar. She wrote down the directions and, then, handed me a piece of paper with her phone number. She said good-bye to us again and said, "We will be there, in case you boys want to go, look for us." We did not go.

I called her five days later. She picked up the phone. "Is this, Rebecca?" I said. "Yes," she replied. This is "Alfredo," I said. "Hi, Alfredo. I thought you would not call. We expected you at the bar," she answered. "I know. I will tell you more about it later when we get together to have a drink or, perhaps, a cup of coffee. When are you free?" I inquired. "Let's meet for lunch, next Monday, it is my day off," she offered. "I tell you what. I want to dedicate my full attention to you without thinking about work. Let's do it on the same day but in the evening. Let's aim for 7pm sharp," I proposed. She agreed. "Let me text you the name of the place and directions to it later today. Secure us a place if you get there before I do and I will do the same, yeah?" I instructed her. "Okay. Call me on Monday morning to confirm," she asked me. "Rebecca, no need to confirm. I value my word. I always keep my promises. However, you can call me if an emergency occurs, otherwise, I will just see you there," I reaffirmed. "Ok. Alfredo. See you there," she concluded. I sent the information I promised her that evening and did not communicate with her until our actual date occurred. I had gone out to eat and have fun with my friends and ended up with a gorgeous date. Isn't that something? When I went out to look for women, I had a hard time meeting them. This time around, I went out just to have fun and I ended up with a date! Go wonder!

Notice how I guided the communication from beginning to end -Total ALPHA energy. The old me would have been eager and desperate about getting to know this woman rapidly. Not this new guy. This new guy was patient and indifferent. She approached me at the table and I did not take my attention away from having fun with my friends.

Just like the cat in my story, she came to our table, teased and tested me, and left again. She wanted my attention. I stayed indifferent and centered. I let her roam around freely. No pressure or special attention. I knew she needed to feel safe around me. I needed to give her the time to finish her discovery of me. Once she felt comfortable, she made her move, by herself. No pressures on either side.

She invited me to meet her at the dancing bar. I did not go. I stayed indifferent. I was not about to leave my friends just to meet with her. No way! That would have meant to her that she was more important than having a fun time with my friends. If she wanted me, she would have to wait for her turn. See, if I would have gone to meet her at the dancing bar, she might think, "I got him." I would appear needy, perhaps even desperate. Since I did not go, I created an unfulfilled expectation or confusion, if you will. I remained mysterious and in control. She probable is accustomed to having guys march to the beat of her drum (BETA energy). Not this guy! This guy marched at the beat of his own drum (ALPHA energy).

She gave me her cell phone number. I did not call or text her right away or the day after. I let her wait to build momentum and anticipation. I called her and I said my name. If she remembered my name it was because her level of interest was high. She remembered me. If she had forgotten my name, I would have ended the call right away. There was no need to force her mind to remember me or the place where we met. That indicated her level of interest was low. My phone call was short and to the point. If I talked to her on the phone for a long time, what would I talk to her about once we met in person? I had to keep mysterious; she needed to discoverer me.

She invited me to lunch. I said dinner. If you do lunch with someone you are barely knowing, is because you have no romantic intentions with them. You eat; then, you have to go back to work. Hell, no! A woman knows that an evening invitation is a romantic invitation. She understands that the person inviting her has an interest in her. She knows that once the dinner and drinks are over, the opportunity for sex is highly possible if everything goes well and the man does not mess it up.

I told her I would text her the name of the place and directions to get there. I needed to earn her trust and confidence with the location we would visit, since it would be the first time we would meet with each other. I knew that once I texted her the information, she would search the place to know more about it. She would then feel secure about the location and be more comfortable with me.

I told her that I am a man of my word. She needed to know she was dealing with somebody mature, one who values his word. Nowadays, it is difficult to find a guy that honors what he promises.

I can be funny and can be mature as well. I needed to communicate that she was dealing with an ALPHA male, a man of essence.

I asked her to secure a table for us. I needed to confirm that she could follow instructions and be on the lookout for me. Could she operate independently? Could she figure things out on her own or did she still need her parents to secure things for her.

I mentioned to her that unless an emergency pops up, I expected her to show up. I did this to verify that either she values her promises, or she is still in the growing up process. Basically, I wanted her to know that I was giving her the liberty to show up voluntarily, without the "confirmation" pressure. If she really was interested in me, she would show up and she would remember the time, date, and location.

I texted her the information I promised her. She texted me three days prior to our date to start a conversation with me via text. I replied with a brief message: "I'd rather answer all your questions personally. So I can see your expressions and listen to your opinions without interruptions. See you then." I did not communicate with her until our agreed date. I had to keep mysterious. I needed to give her time to discover me little by little. She needed to earn my time. Over texting and over calling is BETA energy, feminine. It shows lack of confidence and neediness. It also projects yourself as a control freak with no friends or nothing special going on in your life; that you are afraid of her being dumped for someone else. It shows that you still need a mother to baby-sit you. If you spew everything about yourself via text or by phone, she has nothing mysterious and fun to discover about you. No more intrigue, suspense, or romance. There is nothing more to talk about if you already did all the talking prior to the date. The date will be boring. She will dump you then. She concluded the call and I hung up the phone.

STAY MYSTERIOUS. Throughout our communication process, I disclosed almost no information at all. I was going to give her the chance to start her romantic story with me. Women like surprises and discoveries. I was not about to kill her romantic fantasy by vomiting everything about me. If she wants me, she must earn me by discovering who I am and what I like. The same is true for me. She is a puzzle I need to solve. I also want to know who she is and what she likes. I want to unveil her face to face. I want to play the game, too.

LET THE GAME BEGIN. So, Where do I find "The One", you might ask. You find The One by answering yourself a simple question: What activities do I really enjoy doing or attending? Soccer, movies, baseball, dancing places, museums, malls, shopping centers, fashion shows, school, karaoke, etc. Once you pinpoint the activities you enjoy the most, act. Nothing has been accomplished by wishful thinking. Attend those activities. Once you are there, you will meet people who enjoy what you enjoy. You will have something in common to talk to her about. People who like karaoke attend karaoke bars and restaurants. People who like church go to church. If you like live concerts, go to concerts. Get the point? Attend the places and do the activities YOU like. You will find what you are looking for there.

The same is true in reverse. If you attend places and activities you do not like, you will find what you are not looking for. If you don't like druggies and you attend events and activities where you know drugs reign, you will bring home a druggy and lots of problems. If you dislike opera singing and you attend an opera concert, you will be bored as hell and will project that energy to women who like opera singing. There is a very high probability that you will not find "The One" there, let alone scoring for the night. You find "The One" by visiting the places and doing the activities you really enjoy.

15

SIGNS

OF

ATTRACTION

SIGNS

OF

ATTRACTION

HOW DO I RECOGNIZE IF SOMEONE FINDS ME INTERESTING? First of all, let me give you a BIG piece of advice my friend Gilbert gave me: "Aim for the best or equal to you, never lower." In other words, if you see a woman you REALLY like, go for it. Especially, if you think she is out of your league, either because she is aesthetically beautiful, wealthier, or has better values and principals compared to yours! These women are tired of intimidating men. They want to meet men, too! You will be surprised how many of these women will accept your invitation to get to know them. They appreciate your DARING, having the balls, to even talk to them, let alone inviting them for a cup of coffee. Brave and courageous men cause them intrigue and curiosity.

CAUTION! Do Not Aim for anything less than you. In the majority of cases, these type of women will lower your life style, your thinking, and gradually lower your life expectations. Their values and principles will not match yours! You won't meet at the same mental level. You will have different priorities. You might think, just like men often do, "once she is with me, I will shape her my way." Why do you want to invest your resources trying to change someone who is not compatible with you? Any experienced man or woman will tell you that human beings hardly ever change their nature. You cannot change people permanently. They are the only ones who can change themselves. You will agree with me on this: They will only change temporarily, then, revert to what is familiar to them, their natural behavior.

Don't demote your expectations! Save yourself some headaches and disappointments; **Aim for better or equal!**

You want attention? Do not give attention! As you go about your life, you come across women daily. Some acknowledge you; others do not. The ones that acknowledge you will give you hints that they hope you will catch. The following are the hints they will send your way as a sign to tell you: "Hey, I am approachable. Talk to me. I find you interesting and I am a little curious about you." I listed the hint list in the order as the hints will occur.

1. **Gaze: It is about her hints, not my hints**

    She will gaze at you if she finds you interesting. Gazing is eye-contact. Let's say you are walking in a grocery store. Suddenly, you see her and she sees you. If she sees you and turns her face around ignoring your presence, quit. She is not interested in you. No more pursuing. She is not into you. She does not find you attractive.

    Now, if you see her and she sees you and you both make eye-contact, then she is receptive to your approach. Her eyes are telling you, "You like me, don't you? I find you interesting, too. Well, if you have confidence, then approach me." Don't shy your gazing away. It is a sign of weakness and lack of confidence, BETA energy. Whoever keeps up with the eye-contact is the dominant party

(ALPHA energy). Whoever deflects eye contact becomes the submissive party (BETA energy). So remember, if she gazes at you and her eye-contact stays with you, she is curious about you. Exert dominance by eye-contact until she, nervously or timidly, if you will, turns her eyes away from you.

Gazing is a tremendous tool. Gazing is a tool to exert dominance, peace, confidence, happiness, teasing, surrender, shyness, nervousness, insecurity, attraction and disinterest, etc. Use it wisely. It works for everything in your life. Eye contact is powerful.

2. **Smile:**

She will smile with you if she finds you friendly and/or attractive. Let's say you smile at her, but she does not reciprocate your smile. If she sees you smiling and denies you a smile by ignoring your, don't push it. Two things are happening. 1. She is mentally or emotionally busy. Problems at work, home, financial, etc. 2. She is not interested in you. She either does not like you or is in a relationship already.

If number 1 is the case, don't pursue her. She will bring her drama into your life, she might even get offended if you smile or talk to her. I know what you are thinking. "Once she is with me, I will give her happiness." Don't do it. Remember the

"Make me happy" story I told you before? A person must be the sole source of happiness before she makes a decision to enter into a relationship. Quit playing savior.

If number 2 is the case, quit. You cannot change her mind if she is not interested in you. Chasing is BETA energy. Furthermore, if she is already with someone you must respect her relationship. No ALPHA male goes around destroying established relationships, because it demonstrates lack of integrity to do so. Besides, there is nothing fun about a really mad boyfriend chasing you around the block ready to beat the beans out of you. If you confront any of these two scenarios, walk away. It is not the right time to talk to her and, perhaps, it's better to ignore her altogether.

THE BEST case scenario. You gaze at her and then you give her a smile. She does the same. She is now reciprocating your initial idea. She knows your gazing and smiling express that you find her interesting. Keep a smirk smile while chatting with her. Watch how she, too, wants to smile back at you. Your smirk smile shows confidence, comfort, and playfulness. Women read that. She is now ready for and will reciprocate your initial "Hi?" She will show you friendliness and would welcome your introductory conversation.

3. **Personal Questions:**

Only a person that is interested and curious about another person asks personal questions. But only an astute ALPHA man knows how to answer personal questions to advance his intended purpose. Thinking that women ask personal questions because they are digging you is a common misconception. Women use personal questions as a measuring tool to size up men. They use this method to establish common areas of interest and compatibility. It is the first test women use to weed-out common and ordinary men from exceptional men. *Personal questions are testing questions.* Either you pass or fail. You want to pass. I will show you how to pass by the following example:

You see her working at a store in the mall. You gaze and smile at her. She reciprocates. You approach her and start conversing. She follows you. After briefly chatting with her, she asks you if "You come here often?" She commences testing you. You need to be astute answering her question. If someone tosses a hot potato at you, what do you do? You throw it back at them. Simple. Average and ordinary men would answer "Yes." Savvy men will answer: "What do you mean by often?" *The person asking questions leads the conversation.* BETA answers questions and follows instructions. ALPHA asks questions and directs conversations.

Average and ordinary men not only answer the question but also puke information not requested. "Yes. I come here all the time. It is convenient. I like the atmosphere. Although, I live nearby I prefer to drive my new BMW to get here. Just got it. Bright gray with interior black leather. It is a nice ride. I love it! My parents are well off and I have a nice job. Make good money, too. There are a lot of people around here. I am a people person, you know. I like going to the movies, too. My friend and I watched the movie "The Ultimate Gift" the other day. It was really good! You would like it. I recommend it. After the movie, we had dinner. Then we went to the beach and blah, blah, blah, blah, blah, blah, and blah." He finally shuts down. Then, you both become quiet and she says: "that's good. Okay. I got to go back to work. If there is anything I can help you with, let me know. I'll talk to you later, okay?" And you say, "Okay. It was nice chatting with you." Sure, it was! For you! If you were to ask her, she will tell you that she almost passed out. She could not wait for you to finish your puking so she can politely say good bye to you and not hurt your feelings.

Savvy ALPHA simply say "Well, it depends how you define often." She answers "Yeah, you come here like every weekend?" ALPHA: "Every now and then. How did you end up here, anyhow?" She: "Well, I was looking for a job. My friend Lauri told me about this job. I came over, asked for an application and applied for it. They hired me and I have been here ever since." ALPHA: "Ever since?" She: "7 months ago. Just while I find something better. I like it here but I don't want to stay here forever, you know." ALPHA: "Oh, so you have bigger plans?" She: "Of course! I want to go school here in town. Graduate and find a good job that pays good money. Get my own apartment and get me a better car." ALPHA: "tell me more?" She: "I want to vacation as well. Maybe take a cruise somewhere. I heard that the Mediterranean cruise is fun. They have a lot of activities while on the ship. My friend says that cruise performers are really good. The food is great and the pools are really nice. Can you imagine? That would be wonderful!" ALPHA "I like your plans." Reaffirm her dreams and goals. Show support. She "Oh, my lord, I forgot I am working. I don't know what happened. I just told you my entire life. I hope I did not bore you with my stuff?" ALPHA "Not at all! Thank you for sharing it with me and for trusting me. Somehow, I have a feeling there is more to the story, am I correct?" She: "Oh, yeah, much more. ALPHA: "I want to hear more of it. When are you free so I can hear it to the end?" She: "Well, I get out by 6pm daily and I am off Mondays. ALPHA: "What is your name, by the way? She: "Desiree. Yours? ALPHA: "Peter. Let's exchange numbers. I will text you the information about a great place to get together to continue this chat." She: "we could do lunch, also?" ALPHA: "I would prefer to listen to your story without interruptions and my phone ringing, it will be more fun, don't you agree?" She: "Of course!" ALPHA: "Let's make it a nice evening. I'll text you. I have to go now. I have another errand to attend to." She: "Okay" ALPHA: "CIAO" Smirk smile, blink an eye, and walk away slowly; don't... turn... back (By the way, this is a true story).

Do you see how the average and ordinary guys acted average and ordinary? The majority of men are this way. I know it; my friends were this way and I used to be one. I made it my point to control the conversation from beginning to end. Listening and then questioning has proven to be so powerful that they have spilled out from my personal life into my business world. By keeping an attentive ear, women will share with you their entire wishes, troubles, and aspirations in their life. They also provide you with the information you need to ask her more questions. Ask the questions and shut up. Let them express themselves.

They will ask you the question of "enough about me. I want to know about you," or "tell me about you." You should say something along the lines of "Sure, but I am curious about blah, blah, blah, help me understand how you overcame that situation?" Get her back on track. Once she says "Oh, No! I am not telling you any more about me until you share something about yourself." You say, "Okay. I'll tell you more once we get together that evening." Stay mysterious. Once you are with her at the evening and she asks you the same question, then you can say "Fair enough. I really enjoy your stories. So you want to know about me?" She: "Yes." ALPHA: "Why would you like to know, I am wondering?" Keep your information short and general. Let her earn the specifics little by little. Your job is to always remain mysterious. Let her discover you.

So, remember, just because she is asking personal questions does not mean she is attracted to you. It means she is testing you with personal questions to find common likes and comparability. Don't puke your personal life on her. Do ask her questions so she can tell you her life story. Become genuinely interested in her conversation and NOT in her face, her breasts, or her body. Quit thinking how you are going to do her. Stay present!

4. You give her your name and she asks for yours

A great way to rapidly identify if a woman has a high level of interest in you is by using the following approach. Let's say you meet a woman in line while waiting for lunch. You do a little chit-chatting with her. You carry a friendly conversation with her and she reciprocates. Then, you ask her for her name: "By the way, what is your name?" If she gives you her name but does NOT ask for your name, she is not interested in you. Don't invest more time with her. Just say "Nice chatting with you, Liza." Don't give her more attention.

Now, if you say, "By the way, what is your name?" and she responds, "My name is Liza, *what is your name?*" you are in the game. She feels comfortable talking to you. She is open for more. By her requesting your name, she is telling you she is opening her door of curiosity for you to discover her. Keep chatting with her. Remember, ask questions leading to an evening date. We'll see what happens after dinner. Remain mysterious.

5. She Asks You For Your Name First

This one is a no brainer. You are talking to a woman and she asks you for your name straight out. She finds you interesting and likeable. She is comfortable moving forward with the conversation. As long as you stay in control, there will be dinner and dessert (if you know what I mean by that). She is showing a high level of interest in you.

6. Physical touching

Physical touching is a high level of comfort. She finds you likeable. She goofs around with you and laughs a lot with almost anything you say. She punches you as if mimicking fighting. She behaves like your "bratty little sister". She hides to scare you, jokes around with you, whines and complains, etc. However, learn to stay centered. Don't be too playful, nor too serious. Stay in the middle. Again, as long as you stay in control, the evening will be delightful and the dessert unbelievable.

3. Attraction (which flowers pique your interest?)

Every day you run across women at the market, mall, movies, restaurants, work, etc. You need to have a process, a way to identify which of these women have some level of interest in and like you. You already have it. Invest your time and energy ONLY with open women who are willing to discover and welcome you. However, you need to discover them before they discover you. You already have the hints, the signs, if you will, to attract the right women.

These hints are powerful. They work. Try them. A woman will give you signs, either welcoming you or rejecting you. They give you signs you can interpret immediately.

What conditions must a woman meet for you to find her attractive? Do you remember The Discovery Table? Well, you need to write down what you expect from a woman. Go ahead and build your ideal girl below.

Process to fill in the table:

1. Fill in the table with the top ten Beauties she must have

2. Select the top five Beauties out of the ten Beauties by priority of importance

3. Select the top three Beauties a person MUST have, and you cannot live without, out of the five Beauties you selected before by priority of importance

THE DISCOVERY TABLE

PRIORITY OF IMPORTANCE = 1, 2, 3, 4, etc...

Priority	Inner Beauties	Priority	Outer Beauties

You have designed your ideal woman now. You know how she must be. Don't settle for less. Don't become complacent. If you act casual, you will become a casualty. Be serious about your ideal girl. There are many women around your neighborhood. Don't just date one woman and settle with the first woman willing to date you. No way! You know that women date multiple men before they make a decision to settle with one. So, do the same. Date many women at the same time. If any one of them asks you if you are with another woman, be honest and say, yes, you are dating other women. Let her know you are desirable and she is competing with other ladies for you. She is not your ONLY shot. If she does not like your approach, explain to her that you are looking for "The One". You are exploring all your options. To find "The One" you need to date many women to pick the best and closest to your expectations. If she still disagrees, let her go. Don't allow anyone, not even your own family, force you into a relationship that does not meet your expectations. Let her go. Avoid chaos. Your life should be drama-free. You need to be calm and serene to locate the woman closest to your expectations.

4. FIRST DATE

Never take a first, second, or third date to top-of-the-line, expensive places. If you do, you are sending a message that you are highly impressed by her and you don't want to disappoint her. She will assume that you have never dated a woman like her. She will presume she must be special to you and, for this reason, you are going out of your way to impress her. You will project neediness and don't want to take the chance to lose her. That's how she will read you.

Don't do that! Treat her as equal to other women. You need to see if she is into you based on what you project or who you are. If you project money, she expects all the goodies money can buy. If you project confidence and, if she likes you, then she expects to get to know you. Money should not be an issue for her. She needs to earn the right for you to consider taking her to high-end places. Remember our conversation from a little while back? Do not place women on a pedestal. Treat them all the same.

Many men want to impress a woman sooner rather than later. They purchase expensive clothes, shoes, jewelry, perfume, etc. Some of them even rent cars just for that particular occasion. They take their first date to luxurious and expensive bars, restaurants, etc. They offer to pay for everything their date consumes regardless of the price and quantity. They might spend their whole check on impressing their date, but they don't care at the moment. If you are rich and unlearned, and you don't care, then you can do that. However, if you work for your check daily, you can only go so many times to these high-end places! By the way, rich and savvy men do not spend their money on just about anything or anyone. They consider whether the investment is worth undertaking before moving forward with it. You will end up broke and without her.

Check out this scenario: This is what happens the majority of the time when you over invest in a person you have barely met. You take her to a top-notch restaurant on the first, second, and third dates. She gets excited and cannot wait to see you next time. She is thinking, "Where is he going to take me this time around?" She is now accustomed to the nice, expensive places. She expects better and better. You ran out of money, so you start taking her to modest places. She feels the downgrading on life style. She makes faces of discontent. Her level of romance and happiness dwindle. It is not exciting going to hole-in-the-wall restaurants or bars. She becomes bored. Suddenly, you are not as attractive nor fun for her anymore. She makes up excuses for not going out with you because you are not delivering at the level you introduced her to in the beginning. She breaks promises and dates. She avoids you little by little. Next thing you know, she dumps you.

You wonder what happened. You invested money, energy, and time with her. You expected for her to become your woman or, at least, deliver sex. You wonder what happened. So do yourself a favor: test your dates by taking them to average places. Find places nearby her house to take her to at the beginning. Besides, she will feel more secure and comfortable going to places within her city. Upgrade your dates by taking her to better places, gradually. She needs to earn the right to these places as you see she is meeting your expectations. You also must ascertain she wants to be with you for who you are, your values and principles, and not by what you have or look like. If she doesn't run away as you are running your test, she is probably seeing you as what you are. Once you discover that she does not mind hanging out with you at these "hole-in-the wall" places, and she is meeting some of your expectations, decide if she will be a temporary or permanent relationship. Again, NEVER take your dates to high-end places right away. Improve gradually. Treat all women the same. They need to earn it to win you.

Don't compromise what you expect from a woman just because she has a pretty face or nice body. Respect yourself. If women want to negotiate your expectations, don't do it. Don't surrender or give up what you expect from the other person. This is important: The best position to negotiate is from the position to be willing to walk away from a great deal no matter how good it is. So, if your dates do not meet your expectations, let them go, walk away and don't turn back. Let them find their match in the world. Let them give other men hell. Let them be another man's problem and nightmare. Your area is drama-free. Let them go. Don't chase. Calmly and maturely, let them follow their destiny.

The first date is only an introduction to explore if a relationship with another person is worth considering and pursuing. It is about discovering if there is chemistry between a woman and a man. It is the initial step to penetrating each other's personal zone. The phase of identifying energy-kind signs emitted by the other person, verbally or non-verbally. It is the opportunity to test your Table of Expectations List with your date. You don't need to waste your time by having five dates with the same woman just to find out that the person you are dating has a masculine energy and what you are looking for is feminine energy! Don't over invest your resources with a person, if the person does not come close to the outer and inner beauty factors you expect from your fantasy woman. You must become very familiar with attitudes and actions, masculine and feminine energies, and how they look like and how you can identify them when they show up.

Ask her subtle questions; then stay silent and listen to her. Play detective Columbo. Ask questions you already know the answer for. See, you need to know beauty, so when beauty shows up, you can spot it right away. Lucky for you, you know what you expect from a woman already. You wrote it down in HER Table of Expectations. You need to know how to formulate questions and what answers you should expect from her, so you know whether or not she might be the right person for you. So learn how to ask her strategic questions. Asking purposeful questions is your number one priority when you are dating someone. For example, if you want to know her position on drug consumption, formulate your question strategically. Look at this: "On my way here, I listened to the news in the radio. There was a heated debate about allowing people to buy Marijuana over the counter. Do you think something like that would ever pass and, assuming it passes, how would people feel about it?" Now, just wait for her answer. If she talks in favor of the law, you know that she is pro-drugs. If you are anti-drugs, this is not the right match for you. If she talks against it and you are against it as well, then there is something in common already. If she remains neutral, there you have someone afraid to take a position on important matters of life. Either way, my point here is to show you to strategically poll-answers, smoothly, without asking the question directly.

The man is responsible for asking questions 20 percent of the time he invests with a woman. The right questions will lead conversations into discovering if the woman displays signs of an ALPHA, BETA, or GAMA energy. Lead her to talk 80 percent of the time and, somewhere in between, answer the subtle questions a man poses for her to address, so he can discover what kind of energy she emits. In other words, a man listens most of the time and almost only talks to ask questions and direct the conversation. You should share as little personal information as possible. If she asks you questions, answer them shortly and vaguely and get back to talking about her. Keep yourself mysterious. The objective here is to discover her. Don't impose your life on her.

Listen to her tone of voice, the words she uses, hand positioning, lips and head movements carefully and determine if she projects ALPHA, BETA, or GAMA energy. The attention is 100 percent on her. Don't turn your head around. You will lose important information. Pay attention to her likes. If she likes paint ball, football or rough sports, you know you have some type of ALPHA energy going on with her. More dating and time will tell you the level of ALPHA energy she really possesses. Listen to her expectations in life. Is she looking for someone to take care of her completely or is she pretty much independent? Determine potential compatibility. Does she have what you are looking for in a woman according to your Table of Expectations? Is she a possible temporary, permanent partner, or an incompatible partner?

A TRADITIONAL DATE involves a visit to a restaurant to have dinner, a bar to have a drink, or a coffee shop to sip on coffee or tea. Talk for a little while and, then, go back to each other's house. Maybe a quick and timid hand-shake; rarely a hug or a kiss. Quite boring, right? So, don't ever do it. You will be perceived as a boring date. I will show you a better, more potent, way somebody showed me.

THE NON-TRADITIONAL DATE. The ALPHA date is more fun. You must be bold to have an ALPHA date. This non-traditional date involves compiling two or three activities in the same day. Let me illustrate with an example I recommended to my friends. They tried it out and have made it their own dating strategy. I will narrate my friend Salomon's story.

Salomon set up a date with a woman he met at a video center. On *the first date*, Salomon met her at a quiet restaurant to avoid interruptions and noise while talking and getting to know her. There is nothing more frustrating than someone or something showing up exactly at the time when something important is happening or being discussed. They had dinner. She had a Margarita and Salomon, a beer. They talked more while enjoying their drinks. Salomon made it a point to be interested in her by offering an attentive ear. During the conversation, Salomon discovered his date likes, among many activities, bowling. When he had a chance, he went to the restroom, pulled his cell phone, and located a bowling center nearby the restaurant. He called and confirmed a good time to get there to play bowl. He leaved the restroom and returned to his table. While finishing the drink, he asked his date, if she is "any good" at bowling. She told him she was. He smiled and asked her if she had one more hour to spare to take a challenge. She asked him what kind of challenge that was. Salomon told her that she will have to wait for 10 minutes to find out. Nothing bad, he told her, all good. She became curious, accepted the invitation, and drove together to the bowling center.

She could not believe Salomon had brought her over to bowl. She was surprised! She told him she was expecting to just have dinner and go back home. Salomon gave her a smirk smile and challenged her to a game of bowling. She happily accepted and told him not to be disappointed if he loses all games. He then told her that he grew up with 3 sisters, so he was not going to shy away from the opportunity to teach a lesson to another woman. They laughed and headed over to the counter to purchase the game. She beat him. Badly! But, during the time they were playing, Salomon goofed around with her, as if she was his **bratty-little sister**. She did not mind and teased him back. She actually said to him, she really liked to be teased.

They finished the game 1.5 hours later. He drove her back to the restaurant where she had left her car. She was excited about her date. She told Salomon she expected a dinner and go home type of a date. She told him this was the first time she had a date very different from the ordinary dates and thanked him. He gave her a smirk smile again.

They arrived to the parking space where her car remained parked. Salomon got out of the car and opened the door for her. She showed him a lady-like smile. Salomon told her that it was time for her to go back home. She agreed. They walked over to and he opened the door of her car and, just before her taking sitting in the driver seat, she turned around, gave him a hug and told him she had a great time. He replied that it had been a great time. She drove away as Salomon stood still watching the car disappear into the distance. And that is what an ALPHA male does to be different from other men. This is an extraordinary date. Be bold! Be different!

So when dating someone, aim to have 2-3 activities in one date. The last activity should always be the most romantic one. The one that leads you into the opportunity to be intimate with her. For instance, you can take her to a restaurant/bar, play mini-golf, and finish by walking on the beach or sitting at a park. This is just an idea. You need to figure out what you like and what she discloses to you to identify potential places to visit. Remain mysterious. Don't tell her what is going to happen throughout the day; let her discover it on her own and allow her the chance to live the experience. Just like Salomon said to his date when taking her bowling: "You will find out in 10 minutes." She became curious. Remember the cat story: women are curious and want to know.

If Salomon's date would have said that she did not have one more hour to spare, that would have meant that she had other things to do more important than him, she did not trust Salomon, or no longer was interested in moving forward into forming a relationship. If she needs to go to other places, let her go, don't hang on to her. If she doesn't trust you or want to follow a relationship, let her go, don't beg or request explanations. Let her go. If she is interested in you, she will make the time to be with you no matter what.

Notice also Salomon could have invested more time with her if he wanted to. He chose to limit his time with her. He sent her home. The embedded message here is this: "we already invested enough time together. I like you, but I am not a needy man. I am okay with or without you. Unlike other men, I don't mind waiting for the opportunity to be intimate with you." Unlike other men, he did not mind her company, but he also don't mind letting her follow her way. His time was important. He valued himself. He was willing to let her walk away if he found it necessary. He controlled himself. If she wanted to invest more time with him, there could be another date. He gave her a chance to miss him!

BIG ADVICE HERE: Cell phones are joining dates more often than not nowadays. You have seen couples sitting across from each other at restaurants. They hardly ever talk to each other. She is carrying a conversation on her cell phone. He, too, sometimes does the same as she does. It is more typical in women. This type of action sends the message that the cell phone is more important than you. It also sends the message that she has you and your time under control to do as she wishes. Don't go for that! Don't allow anyone to ignore your presence if they are communicating with you. If your date does not give you the respect you deserve nor value your time, let her know how you feel about it. Don't become complacent. Defend yourself. It sucks to visually wander around while the other person handles her business on the line disregarding your presence. If you allow her to disregard you once, she will make it a habit. Habits are difficult to break once they become deeply rooted inside the person. You will become of less and less importance to her compared to the cell phone and other people, someone of inferior essence.

I have experienced this behavior on several occasions with several women, especially, on the first and second dates. This attitude has become a social epidemic! We have allowed this behavior to pass unnoticed. Not me. I stop them short; even before they have a chance to think about their cell phone. I tell them: "Mary, I value our time together and I want to listen to everything you want to share with me. If you hear my phone vibrating, don't worry, I won't pick it up. I do not want anyone to disrespect this moment. Fair enough,

Mary?" At first they look confused. They don't know what to think or how to answer! Then, they agree, but still look confused... you can see they are thinking that you are a different type of a man! They take you more seriously.

On one occasion, one woman ignored my pre-recommendation. She probably thought I was playing with her. She was goofing off and texting with someone else while I talked to her. We couldn't carry a serious conversation or even stay on topic. I found myself reminding her about the topic at stake constantly! Unpleasant. So I told her that if she had an emergency to attend, I would be okay if she wanted to continue some other time with our date, so she could handle that emergency at once. I knew it was not an emergency. She said she will be okay with that as long as I was okay with it. I told her that emergencies are emergencies and she needed to handle hers. I assured her that we could get back together once we are under less pressure and can control our schedules. She agreed. I cancelled dinner, which she did not appreciate, paid for the beverages, and we parted our own way. I have not heard from her since; nor do I need to! She was not that important. Let someone else deal with her. A week later, I was dating someone else already.

Some women make for awesome dates. They genuinely want to get to know you well and respect you and your time. They want to have a great time with you, some just want to have a good time, if you know what I mean. Other women are just looking for a free dinner because nothing great is going on their lives. They figure, I might as well be in a restaurant checking guys out on someone else's dime than staying here at the house bored and solo. *In a relationship, just like in life itself, you don't get what you deserve; you get what you are willing to negotiate for.*

16

TEMPORARY VS. PERMANENT RELATIONSHIPS

One of my friends gave me some advice that has proven to be extremely valuable. He told me there are two types of relationships. One is temporary and the other one is permanent. My objective is to determine, early in the game, if the woman I am dating is a temporary or permanent partner. We all know a temporary partner is someone we are with just to satisfy sexual desires. We only want to penetrate her physically. It is a person we should not take seriously or be delusional with. There are multiple terms to identify a temporary partner: a friend with benefits or FWB", "a fuck-buddy, sex friend, hook up, casual sex, booty call, a lover, etc. Two people getting together for a carnal favor.

Some temporary relations are exclusive and others inclusive. Exclusive meaning the two friends involved in a relationship can only have sex with each other. They agree to not have intercourse with anyone else. Some people do it for protection, while others want to kick their relationship up one more notch, just to see how things work out. Often times, these relationships convert into a permanent relationship aiming toward moving in together.

The inclusive relationships are open to be intimate with other people. A woman can be doing Peter, John, and Paul at the same time while also doing Tony, the more consistent fuck-buddy. Tony knows his partner is sexually active with multiple partners. He does not care. She is free to do as she pleases. Tony, on the other hand, is doing the same thing as her Fuck-buddy. She does not care. She has no serious ties to Tony. They only get together when they need each other's body.

On the other side of the token, a permanent relationship can also be exclusive and inclusive, just like the example above. The inclusive partners want to stay with their existing partner for a long time, sometimes until they marry another person. Although, they have committed to a permanent relationship, they still want to keep their options open by dating and hooking up with other people.

Now, the permanent exclusive relationship is more meaningful and special. They only care about dating and having sex with each other. They are not interested in multiple partners. At this stage, both people commit to each other and then move in together; sometimes as a lawfully married couple, other times just a voluntary move in situation. These people see themselves more as a comparable couple. They have found some chemistry between each other. They are having fun and hook up often. Usually, their ultimate goal is to marry and create a family.

Thus, my friend told me to determine if the woman I am dating is a temporary or permanent partner, exclusive or inclusive. And I needed to find out, if possible, before the second date. He says I needed to look into the economic and time impact in my life. He told me that I should not spend a lot of my resources in a temporary relationship, regardless if it is inclusive or exclusive. Why invest on top-of-the-line restaurants if you know you are not planning to keep her. You take the temporary dates to small time economical places. Have fun with her cheaply. You know that very shortly either she or you will drop out of the relations. Your investment will be out the window when that happen. And then, what?

My friend, you take the **permanent and exclusive** partner to top-of-the-line restaurants. However, don't do it on the first, second, or even third date either. Let her earn the right to be with you at these top-of-the-line restaurants or places. You have to invest resources with this permanent woman to really get to know her. Eventually, you both will end up together, if everything works out. If you picked right, you will be happy with your relationship and so will she. So, before you start blowing money left and right, find out if she is a temporary or permanent partner. Do it on your first date, but no later than the 3rd. date. If she is neither temporary nor permanent, then drop her all together. Let other guys waste their time with her. Move on and don't look back.

A Straight Dump partner is what it sounds like. A person we want nothing to do with. It does not matter how she looks. We simply clash in energy and have nothing in common. It is the person we forget about and never want to go back with for whatever reason. Sometimes, during the first date, we discover that we feel uncomfortable with the other person. For whatever reason, it just does not feel right.

Well... that's the person you dump and never see again. She also has the right to find her match. Don't stop her.

Single Moms

During your first date, you should confirm if your date has children. Some men want to have and raise their own children. Other men are open to raising another man's children. Luckily, you are the only one that can make that decision. I have ample experience in both routes myself. My first wife and I made and raised our own children. In my second relationship, I did not bring children into it, but my partner did. Then she and I made more children together. Three different ways of living a family life. So before you continue to invest your resources on a woman, determine if you are willing and able to accept her with or without children, for a temporary or permanent relationship.

If the relationship is temporary, then don't worry much about forming a family relationship with her and her children, just have a good time with her. When either of you gets tired of the other, simply end the relationship and move on. Don't form bonds with her children if you know you will leave them eventually. Don't hurt the children with false actions and perceptions. Don't give them false expectations which will break their heart once you both break apart. False hope. If possible, don't even meet the children. Do your thing away from them or when they are not home. You also don't want them to see their mom as a loose woman. Give her and her children respect. Let her safe face with her children. It is only fair the children.

Now, if you decide on a permanent relationship, then decide on whether or not you will welcome her with children. Let me share the possible consequences of your decision. If you decide to procreate and raise your own children, then you will be the biological father. As a biological father, you have full responsibility and control over your children. You decide the life of your children from beginning until they leave the nest. You supervise, discipline, guide, educate, reprimand, feed, clothe, and protect them. You also pass along your values, principles, and mannerisms the way you want to. They submit to you. If at any given time any one of your biological children does not want to follow your teachings, you have full right to set her/him straight. You own the right to set them straight.

Now, many times the mother will interfere and protest while you are applying a correction. You have the right to tell the mother to support you on making sure that you both are educating the children together. She understands you are the biological father. She knows you do not have an ulterior motive to discipline her children. She has no reason to believe you dislike your own children. Therefore, more than likely she will support you. When you have your spouse's support, you also feel more certain about yourself and about the application of your actions as a husband. No stranger can come over and tell you they do not agree with the way you are raising your children. You have total control on your children's up raising. You also eliminate third-party participants. Your wife does not create a mantra that you abuse her children.

For this reason, too many people have decided they want to join someone without children. They want full control as the head of the house and their environment for the children. They want total freedom to pass over to their children principles and values without trying to justify their ways to satisfy others. Personally, this is the best position to be in.

If you decide to raise another man's children, then you will be the father-figure. Don't take this father-figure lightly. Be a great male role-model for her children. As a non-biological father, you have limited responsibility and control over her children. When you accept a woman and her children, you also accept their history, their values, principles, and mannerism they bring along with them. The majority of the time, their values, principals and mannerisms will not match yours. It will become conflicting for you. As you oversee them growing up or once they are living with you, you can change the way they live, talk, view the world, how they treat adults and their parents, their beliefs, and how you want to mold them for the type of family you want to create. Once you discover they are not cooperating and participating in your vision, you try to reprimand them. Now, if the children are 1 or 2 years old when you accepted them, maybe you can mold them to your ways. However, if they are over the age of 3, it will be more difficult for you to build them up to your expectation. If you reprimand them, they will become defensive. They will challenge your authority openly. If you try to guide and teach them you are the authority in the house, and show them the consequences for their acts, they look at mom, run towards mom, seeking refuge with her. The majority of the time, mom will stick up for her babies. You will mellow down, even if you tell her to support you with her children to show them the consequences of their acts, mom would think very carefully before releasing her children to you. Your authority decreases the more children seek her protection. The more she will challenge your application of consequences. She will lean more toward her children. Her mentality is that she can let go of you, but cannot let go of her children. It is usually the mentality of the majority of us, women are not the exception. Her children come first, not you.

If you discipline her child, the child will hold a grudge toward you. Suddenly the child does not want to talk to you, becomes disrespectful, ignores you, and there is little you can do about it. You will try to punish that behavior again. Mom will question you. You try to justify to her, again, the reasons for disciplining the child. She will challenge your reasoning. You will try again to justify your thinking. She will disagree with your reasoning and method. You keep quiet in disbelief. She will tell you to do whatever you want. You will feel guilty about doing anything else to or for the child. Gradually, you retract as a father figure. Little by little, your woman will start to shape your behavior.

Once she has shaped your behavior, slowly, she starts calling the shots on what happens on the child's discipline and life; and eventually in the house. Children are very astute. They know who is the weakest point in the relationship. The majority of the time, mom is the weakest point. Children will turn towards her for protection. They figure "she will care more for me than this other guy. She is easier to convince. She is my mother. This other guy is my mom's boyfriend." At that moment, the children themselves will start to act disrespectfully towards you. You try to discipline them and they will ignore you. Be tough with them, you might get in trouble with the law. Mom will always stick up for her children. The children will use mom as a parapet to show strength and control.

Now, let's say that the mother allows you to discipline her children. IF the biological father is not in the picture, no problem. You have the mother's support. The child will learn to respect authority. But, what about if the father is in the picture? As soon as you discipline the child, the child will cry to her biological Daddy. She will complain about your method of disciplining the child and her disagreement with it. If the biological father is appreciative and rational, he will understand discipline is simply a great way to show consequences and help people advance in the right direction.

However, the majority of the time, this is not the case. Usually, EXs struggle with the concept of other man disciplining his child. The biological father calls mom to complain about her allowing her new boyfriend disciplining his/her child. Mom tries to defend you and your acts. She tells the Ex you have the right to guide the child correctly. The Ex tells her that if his child complains to him one more time about discipline, or that if his child is not being treated nicely and according to his expectations, he will take legal action or meet you face to face. She tries to reason with him. He becomes argumentative. Mom becomes frustrated and upset and turns toward you for understanding and support. Now you have to deal with the Ex as well. You cannot do anything to or for the child because the Ex will either take you to court or will show up to your house, knock on your door, and demand that you both need to talk, as if you were a little kid and just to tell you he does not appreciate your way of disciplining his child. Once the Ex gets in the picture and the Ex starts to participate on how you live your life with his Ex and his child, you stop living your ideal life. You start to live your life based on someone else's expectations. Some other guy dictates the rules and ways to go by. Thus, you become somebody else's child or "doormat."

You make the decision to remain peaceful and careless with the child. You, gradually, start to step out from being a father-figure for the child. Your woman notices your detachment. She tells you she does not appreciate you ignoring your responsibility to be a father-figure to her children. She will question your manliness. She will tell you she needs a man to help her raise her children correctly, involved with their discipline, upbringing, education, etc. In her eyes, everything that is happening is your fault. Because you are weak and do not know how to handle this difficult situation.

Now, the children know you are tangled up between the Mom's frustration and the Ex's threats. The children have created and now have leverage against you. Basically, if they want to go to the movies, the child calls the Ex and the Ex calls your woman to complain about the prohibition placed on his child to go to the movies. The mother will try to explain the situation. He will not understand. She will become frustrated and angry and seek you out. You will become angry with the Ex. You would try to console your woman and, just so you don't have to see the children in your house, you lift up the prohibition and drive them to the movies yourself. You become the children's chauffer.

At that moment, you are no longer the king of your domain, you become a servant to other people, a doormat, I call it. So if you are planning to accept another person with children, consider the consequences. I am not saying that getting together with a single mom is a bad thing. I am saying we need to consider the future consequences when accepting a woman and another man children. They come with different principals, values, and mannerisms, different from yours. The only one that will pay the price here is YOU and ONLY YOU. Like I have said before, you decide how you want to live your life. You decide what type of a relationship you want to build.

One last point here. What about if your woman brings children with her and you both procreate your own children? Briefly, I share with you a fact: UNFAIR TREATMENT AND DISCRIMINATION. Let me illustrate this story.

When my girlfriend and I got together, she brought with her children from another relationship. She expected me to treat her children as my own children. I was willing to do so. Her children were over the age of 7 years old. They were in touch with their biological father and saw him two weekends per month. The children lived with us the rest of the month. So, for those months, my girlfriend wanted me to be a father-figure for them. I accepted this responsibility gracefully. Getting them up in the morning and driving them to school. Homework help. Weekend trips. You name it. My girlfriend wanted us to bond as a family. The children and I pretended we bonded, but we knew we did not. My girlfriend new it also, and she played along with us. At all costs, she wanted me to be her children's father-figure. I couldn't do it. I did not feel it. I became friends with her children, but not a father-figure. We had different expectations and ideas about how to form and behave as a cohesive, functioning family

(Father, mother, children). We clashed little by little. Thus, her children and I created resentment toward each other.

Then, my girlfriend and I procreated a baby. From the very day my baby was born, I naturally sought bonding with her. I hugged her and kissed her. Gently bit her soft cheeks. I talked to her tenderly, even when I knew she did not understand my words; I felt as though she understood my fatherly-love for her. It became a natural instinct for me to act father-like. Then I heard the first complaint from my girlfriend. She said how come I could not express my love to her daughters in the same fashion as I do for my baby. I told her that this was my baby. Something biologically within me tickled me to act and express my feeling freely, lovingly even. I told her I couldn't explain it. It's different.

I tried to participate equally in all of our children's activities. For some odd reason, my daughter, now 5 years old, offered me more emotional satisfaction. Her accomplishments, at home and at school, were more meaningful to me. I was happy seeing my girlfriend's children participate at school plays and graduations. I was happy with their performance. I would hug them and congratulate them. But the graduation of my biological child gave me a sense of accomplishment. I would hug, kiss her, laughed with her, and swung her around me with ecstasy. My girlfriend would tell me how come I was different with her daughters. I repeated: "Something within me tickled me to act and express my feeling this way." I told her I couldn't explain it. It's different.

The children expected for me to participate equally in their lives. I tried. I asked my step-children to do homework. They thought it was stupid and I did not push them daily and consistently. However, my daughter will not go to bed until she had completed all her homework daily and consistently. I pushed her. I could not take a NO from her. For some reason, my brain, heart, and my emotions expected a superior performance from my biological daughter. My girlfriend's family noticed this difference and she let me know about it. "How come you do not push all the children the same as you push your daughter?" she would complain. And I used to tell her that "something within me tickled me to act and express my feeling freely." I told her I couldn't explain it. It's different.

Nevertheless, I tried treating all of the children as my own children. I wanted to be a father-figure to all of them. I provided the same advice for them all. But, I could not express my emotions with them all equally and freely. See, I could hug, kiss, bite my daughter's cheeks anytime and anywhere I felt like it. I could be playful and warm with them without thinking that somebody would get the wrong idea about my playfulness. I placed my daughter on my lap disregarding the people around us to listen to her little stories. It just did not feel the same with my girlfriend's children. Don't get me wrong. They were good children.

But, for some reason, my heart leaned more toward my daughter. I told her I couldn't explain it. It's different. Blood is just thicker than water.

The point of this story is this. When you decide to move in together with a single mom, and between you and her, procreate a child, you will be tested on unfair treatment and discrimination. You need to decide if this type of relationship is an option for you prior to committing and entering into a relationship. Once you are in it, you will have to deal with your own blood and the blood of another man. She does not have this dilemma; both children are hers! Will you treat them equally? Again, only you can decide what's good for you. I tried it. I ended up with a bad taste in my mouth. I am not saying these types of relationships are bad, I am saying you need to be aware of your options and consequences.

5. Discovery Process

Now, you are in the discovery process. This process is pivotal. Don't forget your Table of Expectations for her. Keep these expectations in mind whether you are or are not with her. You will have to check-mark expectations she meets and expectations she lacks.

Select the right person from the beginning. If you don't, you will be in trouble later as the relationship grows. It is emotionally painful to terminate a long-term relationship. Almost all divorces nowadays happened because both, men and women alike, more specifically men, fail to identify the expectations they envision for a woman. Many times men don't even know what they are looking for in a woman. We just see a face, boobs, butt, vagina, and sex! Then, they move in together. Months later after living together, they gradually discover that the person they are with is not the correct person for them. Relationship disagreements and problems follow and they become roommates. Once tired of each other, separation confirms their failure to pick correctly from the beginning. **Date multiple women during the same period**. Again, just like women do, date multiple women at the same time. Don't you care what people say or think about you? You are the only one who will face the consequences of your acts, not others, at the end of the road.

Some people ride the ride and keep their relationship going, even if they hate living with their partner. Other people terminate the relationship after surrendering many years of their youth and resources. For this reason, it is better to avoid entering into a relationship early in the discovery process and not months or years later. The discovery process is for you to weed-out women that are the least compatible with you. Don't feel bad or take it personal once ending a relationship. Feel bad if you don't! Don't deprive her from finding the man she deserves. You need to focus on finding the woman who deserves you and you deserve. AGAIN, keep your Table of Expectations in mind. Save frustration, disagreement, tears, and time! **Date multiple woman at the same time**. Again, just like women do, date multiple women at the same time. Don't you worry about what people would say or think about you. You are the only one who will face the consequences of your acts, not others. This repetition is not a mistake. It is an additional reminder.

The discovery process is for you and her to get to know each other. Going to the beach, parties, attending events, being playful, and discovering each other's character and likes, values, beliefs, morals, foundations, expectations in life as a person, dogmas, family views, everything that has to do with each other. The more you know about her early in the game, the better off you will be to make a sound decision when the time comes to consider her worthy or not for a temporary or permanent relationship; heck, it might even be a straight dump!

If you think you are the only person in the relationship applying a discovery process while dating, you are wrong. Women have trained themselves, from an early age, to size up men promptly. They have an automatic switch that turns on their instincts and ideas. As soon as a man makes verbal or non-verbal contact with them, the switch goes on. Anything you say to a woman, she will find a meaning for it. She will be analyzing you and your mannerisms all day long. Don't feel guilty about running your Table of Expectations on her as well. Do not feel bad about testing a woman; feel bad if you do not! Because she is testing you, boy!

Discovery Process Communication.

Let's assume you have finished your first date. Both of you are happy about the date results. Men, don't tell her you had a great time with her. Wait for her to tell you she had a great time with you. If she does not mention it, you don't bring it up either. When she departs away from you, you will be tempted to send her a text message. Don't do it. Let her send you the text message. Once you receive her message, reply to it 2 or 3 hours later. Most likely she will tell you she had a lot of fun with you. You should respond with something along the lines of "I am glad to hear that!" She WILL be expecting to read in your response that you want to have another date with her. Don't do it. Give her a break. A simple "I am glad to hear that!" is enough. Allow her to wonder whether or not she was a good date for you. She will respond to your response if you had a great time with her? Answer back the day after. Start aiming for the second date by saying that you will tell her the details next time you both get together. Leave it at that. She will text you more to get the information she needs from you. Tell her you are busy right now and cannot address her question via text, but you will answer it next time you both get together. She will get the point that you are not needy but you are a busy person.

Keep your communication to the point and very, very short. You must remain mysterious. She needs to have some type of mystery to aim for and discover. Whether or not you both have another date, it is a matter of time. So don't tangle yourself up by over communicating with her via texting, email, social media, phone calls, etc. You don't initiate any of these activities. You wait for her to initiate these activities, and once she initiates them, you address them shortly and to the point aiming for the next date with her.

If you have any social media contact, (Facebook, Twitter, Instagram, etc.) don't publish anything about you and your activities. Read what others do, but keep your mystery intact. She will go mad because you are not volunteering, as almost ALL men do, information she is looking for about you. Let's say that, by mistake, one of your friends posts a picture of you in a boat in the ocean. Once she sees it, she will ask you about it. Just tell her that you can talk about it next time you both get together. That is what you do in case she becomes curious about anything related to you on social media. You will tell her more about it face to face. Again, women love mystery. Women want romance and to discover a man.

Your job, as a man, is to keep the mystery going. Any time she emails, texts, Twitters, don't reply right away. Men with goals and ambitions are busy and dedicated to their purpose. They don't have time to chit-chat or gossip with people. They are busy working on their purpose and advancing their goals. Their time is valuable. They prefer to handle matters personally.

If she wants to know about your day, reply to her 2 to 3 hours later: "Busy day! You probably are busy, too. When are you free to get a drink?" and that's all you have to say. Move on. She might even demand an explanation from you as to why you did not to answer her messages promptly or your reply was too short. Be clever with your response. I usually tell them that "I have goals and projects I am working on daily. These goals and projects depend on my dedication and concentration. They depend on me. Besides, when you talk to me I want to dedicate my full attention to you, only. When I am with you, face to face, I want no one to bother us. It is our time. Fair enough? So, when are you free to have a toast for us?" Don't copy these answers. You need to find the answers that mimic your personality.

Now, if she does not reply to your message, don't text her again. You are playing ping-pong with her. Once you hit the ball over to her court, she needs to send it back to you. It is okay for her to take her time to return the ball to you. You are not needy, desperate, or in a hurry sweating bullets because she does not return the ball. Give her time and liberty to play, too. Now, if she does not return the ball at all, move on. If you are important to her, she will return the ball eventually.

When she does, be indifferent and don't demand explanations. You just have to say: "great to hear from you. Let's get together one of these days so we can catch up. Text me Friday all the details?" Leave it at that. You want her to text you to confirm she is genuinely interested in getting together with you. Give her a specific day to text you. People remember important days, if they are important. If she remembers, set a time for the next date. Never accept a date on the same day she proposes a date. Busy, goal-oriented men have to organize their schedules. They are all busy! If she plays busy, don't chase her, needy men chase, just tell her to "let me know once you know your schedule." Wait until she gets back to you. Keep mysterious, unneedy and busy. Keep indifferent.

If she agrees to a date with you, meet her at a location nearby your place. Don't drive a long distance for her. She needs to earn that compliment from you. Don't take her to dinner or a bar. Take her for a drink or a cup of coffee. Refresh your memory with your Table of Expectations for her. Start the game over. Give her a chance to prove her interest in you.

Now, if she has visited your house before, just invite her to come over to your place and cook dinner together. She must come to you or there is no date. Allow her to invest efforts into winning you back. Yes, you heard me right. She is the one that dropped the ball. She needs to earn points to win you back. If she refuses to make dinner with you, let her go, permanently. There are many women in the world. Don't chase her. Next.

So keep mysterious. Don't tell her where and/or how you both are going to enjoy your date. She will ask you about "the plans for the evening?" That is for you to know and for her to discover. She will be insistent by saying that she needs to know what to wear for the occasion. Just tell her to dress casual or formal. If you are taking her to a nice dinner place, tell her to dress to impress. Now, if you are just going to the mall or the beach, tell her to be casual, open-toe shoes will be just fine. She will be insistent. You assure her that she will enjoy the evening. How do you think she is feeling just about now? That's right! That's what you want.

She will go crazy until the day and time she experiences your promise. She will talk to her friends about this "mysterious man" and her "nerve-wracking" dates. Her friends suddenly would become curious about this mysterious man. They want to know what a Mysterious man looks like, if they don't have one next to them (which is most likely their case). After the date, you can bet that her friends would want to get the scoop regarding your date. It is fun to see your lady become the center of attention while she talks about you. She will love you for that!

What is happening here? Well, you are building up momentum and anticipation. Her days prior to her date, become too long and will kill her softly. She becomes anxious about her Friday's date. She needs to get together with you. Little by little, you are giving her the opportunity to experience romance on your terms. Don't puke, like almost every man does, you are going to start at point A then B then C. Don't ruin her emotional experience. Don't tell them about the movie! Keep the movie a secret! Keep her wondering. She will be frustrated. Deep inside of her, she is loving it. It is a hate-love emotion.

WARNING: Use your technology devices wisely. Don't over message, text, or call her. Don't become her gossip buddy. The person she contacts when she is bored. The guy she already knows everything about. The one she can just call and would puke his guts out to keep her entertained. Don't become her counselor and savior. Girls love to talk. It is their nature. Gradually, she will push you over and treat you as just another friend. You are not a challenge to her any more. You are not mysterious any more. You are boring now. There is no anticipation. No discovery. She already knows what you are going to do next. No intrigue, no fun!

More importantly, she needs reassurance accepting you are not a needy, dependent guy. You want her to know you are a SPECIAL man. You are important. Your time is valuable. You are worth the waiting for. So, keep busy, interesting, and mysterious. Use phone calls, texting and messaging as a way to set up your next date. Don't fall into the trap of "let's just be friends." She is either your girl or no friendship. Next thing she will ask you for is for you to become her personal handyman while other guy is having sex with her. Keep her wondering. Create anticipation. Keep her anxious. Let her experience her emotional roller coaster. Allow her to fulfill her romance by discovering who you are. Let her earn time with you. She will value and appreciate YOU more.

Relationship Courting:

You have found your woman now. The process of courtship begins. When you are courting a woman, you are going to invest time, energy and your hard-earned money. Courtship is the period of time people use to develop the interest to marry or develop a romantic relationship. Courtship is the opportunity a couple has to write their own romantic novel. It is the period a man has to persuade his woman to fall in love with him. It is the time for a woman to experience her romantic journey, to experience fantasies and curiosities, with her "Prince Charming." Essentially, it is the period of time which would determine if two people belong to each other to consummate a long-term relationship.

It is true that courtship is the time we have to romance a woman. Everybody knows that! However, my take and focus on courtship is different. Courtship is the opportunity a man has to test and affirm that the person he is dating and courting has the qualities he is looking for. Your Table of Expectations for her becomes extremely valuable at this stage. Check mark expectations she does not fulfill. See how many of your expectations she REALLY possesses. If you expect her to have integrity, place her in scenarios where her integrity will be tested and observe her performance. Testing her?! Yeah! She is testing you all the time, too! If she fails on integrity, give her a bad check-mark. If she disrespects you as a human being and partner, give her a bad check mark. You get the picture.

I am dropping a BOMB right here: Courtship is for you to establish how consistent she is with her behavior and the honor she places on commitments. Discover how she behaves in public and around friends. Too many people suffer from behavioral disorders. They are happy one day and angry the next. She is happy to have dinner with you and, once she arrives to the restaurant, she becomes moody. She tells you to pick her up at 5pm and disappointed because you arrived at 4:50pm. She is watching other people while you are chatting with her. She tells you she will do one thing and does another. She calls you at the last minute or simply not show up to meet with you. What you see is what you will get. Hear what she says and, more importantly, WATCH WHAT SHE DOES. Actions are the facts that really matter.

Courting exposes a person suffering from behavioral problems. It also provides an excellent opportunity to confirm when a woman is loyal to her commitments. She does what she says she will do all the time. From my experience, a woman that does what she commits to all the time, is a woman of honor. She is heads above almost every woman. They are rare, but they exist. This is the woman every man envisions. And courtship is the vehicle to select the greatest from the best partners. Don't you be afraid to HOLD HER ACCOUNTABLE TO A HIGHER STANDARD! You deserve the best partner possible. This is the perfect period to either establish a long-term relationship, a fuck-buddy agreement, or a straight dump. Don't be afraid to pull the trigger on either one of the choices! It is what it is!

The majority of men see courtship as the opportunity to impress a woman. They take a girl out to the movies, play mini-golf, to the beach, to dance, nice restaurants, comedy shows, gaming, traveling, partying, bars, picnics, camping, museums, malls, etc., etc., etc. This is what courtship is about for the great majority of average, ordinary and uninformed men. This is what women expect from every man. ALPHAs do not aim at impressing other people, they expect for other people to impress them. For us, it is about doing what is expected in a courtship and more. We have a high standard. We expect more from women. We want to romance what is meaningful and valuable. We want to invest our time, energy and money with a person that meets our expectations and deserves to be with us, the ones that have character and integrity, sound principles and values. Women unwilling to be average and ordinary. Feminine women comfortable in their skin! They deserve us!

Courtship is precious to an educated ALPHA male. He gets only the best from the better. Many women do not deserve us and you don't want them either. Let them go. Let other men deal with them. Let the uneducated, average and ordinary, men waste their time, energy and money with them. Let other men do what is ordinary, common, and expected. ALPHA males do not do what is common, ordinary or expected. They do the opposite. In this case, the process of courtship is to get to know the person and give her a good time. It is the only period a man has to assess that the woman he is dating brings value to us. For us, courtship is about finding out if a woman honors her commitments, honors her man, and has solid principal and values.

Sure you want to take her out for an ice cream, walks on the beach, hug and kiss her, just like expected. Everybody knows that! What almost no one knows is that, every time you are hugging, kissing and taking her out for dinner, you are studying her. You want to know if this person is consistent with her behavior, what family foundation she brings with her, principles and values. Aside from her exterior beauty, what else is she bringing to the table? Is she the quality of a person you want to have on your side. More importantly, is she mother material, the type of a mother you expect for your children to have.

See, my friend, don't just go for the looks and for what society expects from courtship. There are many beautiful women everywhere you look at. You look at one and the other and everyone is beautiful in their own way. There are so many beautiful women in the world. For this reason, all of them are the same; what make them different is the way they think.

Too many men screw up right here. They have a pretty woman and they fear losing her. They will cry rivers to retain her because "she is so pretty." We, the informed ALPHA males, appreciate beauty but are more interested in inner beauty, their essence, and the core of the person. We are interested in values, principals and foundations. So, hold women to a higher standard so you can have the better from the best. For you to have the best, you must hold yourself to an even higher standard!

6. Falling In Love

Never propose to anyone to move in together while you are in love with the person and never propose marriage to any one if you are in love with that person! Especially, if your heart and guts are telling you: "This is the ONE. This is the ONE." Don't listen to the little voice inside you, just yet! Do not do it. It is the worse time to make that kind of a decision. It is not the real you making that proposition. It is the person you try to be for her. You are thinking with your heart, your emotions and feelings! Not logically. At this time, the world is rosy and marvelous and is perfect. The flowers smell great! We see no evil and hear no evil. Everything looks good. We even think that the pimple on her forehead makes her look kind of cute. We become and behave child-like. We ignore the obvious, because we are extremely concentrated in the butterflies inside our body and calid obsession and sexual attraction feelings we experience every time she is near us. We are willing to sacrifice everything for her. She is everything to us. We are extremely emotional and optimistic. We feel we can carry the world on our shoulder and that we can defeat anyone or anything just for her. It is amazing how a person that has fallen in love can be transformed emotionally and psychologically.

See, the majority of people in the world follow the universally accepted idea to get married when you are in love. The movies, television, and the printed media have done great programming women and men alike to commit to a life-long commitment while emotionally intoxicated. She is in love and so is he. Together they will conquer the world. He is the ONE and so is SHE. That is a major mistake to make.

Never assume that the attitude and energy we fell in love with will still have the same intensity 1 or 2 years later. See, you don't know the reality of a person until you live with her 24/7/365, non-stop. Divorcees agree they made decisions too quickly and in the heat of the moment. They did not take the time to REALLY get to know their partner. Divorcees will also tell you that the reason for their divorce is because their partner gradually changed attitude over time. They discovered the REAL attitude and energy of their partner and desired not to put up with it. The energy they should have uncovered before declaring marriage commitments. For this reason, I say, and too many people will agree with me, that entering into a commitment when you are in love is just plain immature, crazy, and unwise.

No woman wants to move in with some one that is madly in love today and after time passes by, regrets having made the decision to have developed a relationship. Any person, man or woman, can tell you they want to get together with someone who knows what he or she wants. No man or woman, likes an insecure, confused person on their side. No one likes to be with or be a person forced into a relationship. That is a recipe for failure. Women want to be with someone they know have made a calm and conscious decision when moving into a relationship. No one likes to be in and out of relationships. No one likes to experience perpetual problems, frustrations, stress, and conflicts. Nobody! Every one of us want to form loving and caring relationships. We want a better life to share our emotions and spirituality, a more fulfilling intimacy. For this reason, women are happy with a man that is himself, a man that has made a conscious decision to enter into a relationship because that is what he logically wanted.

No man or woman wants to go into a permanent relationship for the sake of sex. If that's your case, you will be better off soliciting the services of a prostitute. If all you want is the warm body of a woman next to you, just to touch her and have sex with her, a permanent relationship is not for you. Sex can become boring! "What?!" you might say. Yes. You heard me right. SEX CAN BECOME BORING, when it is abused.

Sex is a spontaneous reward we give to and receive from our partner, not a habit. When we make it a habit, intimacy loses its value and essence; it loses its flavor and mysticism. It becomes work. Tedious, forceful, and unfulfilling work. Touching and kissing her feels odd, almost as if you are bothered by that. On bed, men play "sleepy" and women play "I have a headache" or "I am tired," because we are too lazy to do what we now consider work. Heck, for some couples sex has become like a penitence. This, in my opinion, is the reason why over 50 percent of the divorces in the world occur. This is why we have so many stressed out and ungratified, people universally.

Once a man or a woman becomes bored with their relationship, they look for new ways to use their time to gain "happiness." They seek other types of gratification, like alcohol, drugs, movies, cheating, friends, etc., once sex no longer satisfy them. Problems, angriness, discontents, arguments, stress, disagreements, disrespect, isolation, cheating or separation will be inevitable. It is just a matter of time before you and her get tired of sex and each other. More of the same brings more of the same. More of the same is monotonous; monotony kills relationships.

Going into a relationship for the sake of having sex with a nice body is a bad choice. You will break someone's heart and, more importantly, you will break yours as well. So, be wise. Don't fall in love with the body, fall in love with inner beauty. Don't commit to any type of relationships, moving in together or marriage, when you are in love. It is not the real you making the decision. Wait until your feelings and emotions settle down. Wait for the hype to cool off. Wait until you regain logic and sense. Only then, you can ask her to MOVE IN with you, not marriage.

I repeat: DO NOT PROPOSE MARRIAGE TO HER. Propose her to move in together, instead! You already know her integrity, mannerism, ideas, and personality from dating her. You have an idea about her public demeanor. Don't you want to know how she REALLY is when she starts to live with you every day? Her private demeanor? Of course, you do! Well, moving in together is the best opportunity you have to discover more about her, prior to committing to legal contract: Marriage.

I know you will disappoint the social dogmas for following unconventional ideas, for following your own desires. Your parents and her parents might become disappointed with both of you as well. If making other people or society mad worries you, let me tell you something: They will not be there with you when you are fighting the fight, stressing out, frustrated, angry, hopeless, hurt or in courts trying to keep what is legally yours during the divorce or separation. When was the last time that any one knocked on your door to volunteer to pay for your rent and your daily life necessities? So, why do you worry about what others think of you or how you go about your business?

The true ALPHA male is willing to stand alone when necessary. If she does not want to move in together prior to marriage, then you have a tough decision to make. For me, this decision is easy to make now: *I won't marry her*, no matter how much I like or feel I love her. I will just become her "friend with benefits" and develop an open relationship. I know you will be tempted to follow her rules about "marriage first." You will think that if you do not marry this woman, you might not find another one like her. That's true. You will find someone that is different, MENTALLY. If she really loves you and **trust** you, she will move in with you regardless of other people's approval. Is she does not trust you, she will refuse to move in with you no matter how loud you cry. Marrying someone, before living with them, is a ritual of the past. Men and women, our society has progressed. We have different expectations from each other nowadays. We have become more open to try things out first. We must make sure that there will be compatibility with each other once we live together. Compatibility is essential to form solid, long-lasting relationships. Moving together is a socially accepted idea now. You must know how she behaves once you share a home with her. The last thing you want is to waste your most valuable resource: TIME. No moving together, no marriage.

7. Move in together

The try out period. Try the relationship out first. Make sure the pool has water before you jump into it. Advice: don't tell her you are testing her. You are the ONLY one that needs to know that. Don't tell her how you want her to be or how YOUR woman should behave. Give her freedom so she can unfold herself comfortably and naturally. Step back and watch her go about her daily business. Hear and, EXTREMELY more IMPORTANT, watch what she does. Allow her to become comfortable with you and the house. Attitude and energy follows. Remember, she needs to feel free to create choices and make independent decisions. The choices and decisions she makes and acts on, will tell you the quality of attitude and type of energy she really possess.

Live with her for at least 1 year. You are free to leave her any time you feel like it with no compromises on either side. It usually takes about 9-12 months for the real person, attitude, and energy to show up in the relationship. You have about 12 months to know her mannerism, habits, mores, hygiene, integrity, passions in life, dislikes, family views, spirituality, on and on. It's until you live with a person you discover her attitude and position in the relationship, how she uses her time and how she sees you and treats you as the man of the house. You have 1 year to compare your Table of Expectations to her real attitude and energy. Only you know when you have found the person you deserve. Only you can authorize if she meets your most important expectations as a woman. Don't feel bad about this process, she is most likely applying the same process to you, too. She just doesn't talk about it with you, but she is definitely talking about you with her girlfriends. Besides, as an ALPHA male, you must know your expectations before jumping into a life-long commitment. Jump in the pool only if you see and touch the water and its depth. Never apologize for having a high standard and expectations for your partner or for knowing what you want in life!

And now that we are talking about moving in together, let me tell you something extremely important: Are you moving into her place or is she moving into your place or both of you moving into a new place? Although this question seems meaningless, it is essential to address before you both decide to move in together.

My friend, Julie, told me she was not okay for her partner to move into her place. "That is not man-like behavior. A man does not move into a lady's place. He needs to have his own place and I can move into his place; ... show he has accomplished some type of independence. I don't want to provide a home for my man. I want to be with a man that can offer me security and protection when things go wrong. I have to be sure that he can carry the torch when things get tough for me. I would even be willing to consider moving in with him into a NEW place to start our relationship fresh," she said. "But, he is not moving into my place," she said. "I want to start fresh moments and memories with him," she added.

I spoke with several men who moved into their girlfriends' place. They wished they would have not moved into their girlfriends' place. They felt underpowered, indecisive, and weak making the tough decisions as the leader of the house. I can agree with them. I am very familiar with this feeling, because I lived it twice. I can still remember those phrases: "This is my house, you can leave any time you want. Why do you make decisions in my house when my name is on the lease?" I tell you, they were humbling experiences.

Here is a BIG ONE: Don't move in with her or your relatives' house. It is simply a bad move. It could be a relationship-destroying move! Everybody will tell her or you how you both should live your life. Both of you will almost have no freedom to do as you please. Your life style and intimacy will suffer. If you want a partner, you need your own place.

Whichever decision you make regarding the best way to move in with your partner, always consider your pros and cons carefully.

However, if this is not possible, there is a much better alternative, which I favor over all choices: move into a neutral house, a new place and a fresh start for both of you. Thus, both enter into a balanced place and circumstance with equality in the house. No one has more authority than the other regarding the house. It belongs to both of you because both you started it together.

17

PRENUPTIAL AGREEMENT

Drop this BOMB as the last check mark! Before you commit to a relationship and before you propose marriage to her, **you need a Prenuptial Agreement**. Once you have found the "The One" person you want to be with, you have one more responsibility to you: CYA! Cover Your Assets. The most basic of these contracts lists an inventory of Pre-Marital Assets that, in the event of a divorce, will remain the property of the original owner. You worked hard for personal belongings, unless you allow another person to take away your assets, no one should have legal rights to despoil you from your assets. Protect your savings, your retirements, your pensions, you mutual funds, your money, your house, your land, your cars, your inheritances, your personal property, and anything you have accumulated by yourself and brought into the relationship. Protect your pre-marriage wealth! It is ONLY yours. Many of us will inherit our parents' properties, monies, life insurance benefits, personal wealth. We must protect them. Our parents worked too hard for it. Once they transfer it to you, it is only for you. You do not need to share it with anyone you don't want to. A prenuptial agreement will help you keep what is rightfully and ONLY yours. Be wise. Be prudent. You owe it to yourself.

Your prenuptial agreement should also include your future as well. If you and your spouse build a profitable business and you split, how are you both going to split the business? If you buy a house, boat, cars and you divorce, what method will you use to accelerate a fair separation of benefits? Prenuptials are not just for celebrities. They are there for everyone who want to protect their wealth. *Prenuptial agreements are for the prudent person.* Before you die, you have the choice to transfer your wealth as you see it fits. But as long as you are alive, you should be the only one in full control of your wealth. See an attorney. Invests pennies and save future thousands.

"I am embarrassed to ask my girlfriend for a prenuptial agreement." Don't be! She won't be embarrassed to take you to court! She will fight you for as many assets as possible. And, if you have children with her, she will create an inferno for you. She might say "a prenuptial agreement? You don't trust me?" And a good response to this question should be "honey, if I become disabled or about to die, probably you will take control of my assets. But as long as I am alive and well, I want to control my assets. Now, together we will create more assets. We can talk and agree about how we can both control the assets we create together." Keep control of your pre-marriage assets until the day your die. Don't be afraid. Be upfront and confident. Ask every divorced man you know, how fun the separation process was, the fight in court, attorney's fees, and how much they kept from the pre-marriage wealth and assets created together while in the relationship. Make sure you have a cup of coffee, because they will tell you A STORY! Don't be embarrassed to defend and protect what is ONLY yours.

I am about to save your life right now. Here is an advice that will help you save anger, frustration, and tears. Once you propose your prenuptial agreement to her and she disagrees with it, she is not coming to you for love. She has secondary motives. Now if she does not objects and happily accepts your agreement, you have found a person willing to be with you for love. No secondary motives, only love. The prenuptial agreement is the last weed-out tool, the last test a woman must pass, in order for you to give her the final approval: "Would you marry me."

8. Maturity (time to marry)

While living together, your relationship has grown and matured, just like a human being grows up to become someone in life. Just like the baby has to overcome challenges, doubts, and obstacles to find meaning in himself, so do couples. They must endure disagreements, angriness, disappointments, shortcoming, and imperfections to find meaning in a relationship. Relationships are like flowers, they come with thorns. If you want the flower, you have to accept the thorns as well. Once a couple overcomes challenges, obstacles, doubts, disagreements, ups and downs, they have created a mature relationship. The logic to propose marriage, now exists.

There was a time when we did not know our partner. Yet, we gathered some courage to talk to her and invite her out. On your first date you discovered that a relationship with your date was worth pursuing. While dating her, you kept in mind your list of expectations and, although she did not meet all your expectations, she met the most important ones. You liked the way she carried herself while dating her. Then you made the decision, logically and not emotionally, to move in together. While living together, you both discovered and managed each other's differences and views on just about everything and kept the relationship meaningful and functional. You opened your heart and mind to treat each other as responsible adults. You drove your relationship to maturity. She has accepted and legally signed your prenuptial agreement without holding anything against you.

Maturity, as the term implies, is simply the process we use to project our comfort with who we are in the relationship and as a person. It says that we have found a way to balance, for the relationship's benefit, differences between two people. Slowly, we become people of integrity, honor our promises, and respect the opinions of our partner. We can communicate as mature adults when disagreements exist and find mutually benefiting consensus, thriving on each other's success and applaud our partner's accomplishments. We always lookout for our partner and promote the relationship growth and, at the same time, ours. Vainness, vanity, put-downs, humiliation, negative pride, do not exist within a mature relationship. Only humility, understanding, up-lifting, sound advice, trust, peace, confidence, appreciation, truthfulness, clarity, honesty, loyalty, love, and solidarity are accepted in a mature relationship. When you have at least these positive factors within your relationship, it is time to propose and marry your partner. Congratulations, you will have a happy and meaningful life. You will be a great example worth for your children and others to emulate.

18

DRAMA-FREE CIRCLE

The objective now is to keep your relationship drama-free. You need clarity and peace. You have invested time, money and energy in building a relationship. You have to build a Drama-Free circle.

This Drama-Free circle should exist even before, in the process of building, during and after building a relationship. If you did not know or did not have a Drama-Free circle, you must make it a point to create it now. The circle exist to protect you, primarily, and your relationship. Imagine the circle to serve you as a shell to protect you from infections capable of bringing you discomfort and damage into you. Everybody needs a Drama-Free circle for protection, just like an egg shell protects its chicken-egg before hatching from exterior viruses capable of killing the unborn chicken.

We all have opinions on just about everything. We offer our opinions even when they are not requested. We give our opinions without malice and hope to participate in the well-being of the person receiving the advice. We want to help them alleviate their challenges. Among these people we have our friends, family, social dogmas, personal challenges, and business acquaintances. Among them, there are people we admire and want to be like. These people are willing to provide their opinion and influence our decisions and our life. They don't mean to hurt you. They want us to be happy. However, many times they don't realize that the advice they give to people adds additional confusion in the decision-making process. It adds additional stress and frustration. The more people offering their opinion, the more confusions. Many times, when giving our advice, we affect people.

For this reason, it is recommended, throughout this book, that a man should have a deep and clear understanding of his values and principles; what he stands for; his expectations in life; factors he is willing to put up with or simply not accept. You should be able to solve your own problems and arrive to your own conclusion without giving people the opportunity to penetrate your Drama-Free Circle and, thus, bringing turbulence into to your life.

We all have friends packed up with their own life problems. Those friends make it a point to communicate their life dramas to us. When they share their dramas with us, unconsciously and indirectly, they dragged us into their problems. They dump their drama on us. They expect an opinion from us. We start to play "**savior**." Thus, we add more foreign drama into our life. Now, we did not expect to part take on this unsolicited drama. We have little or nothing to do with it. And, yet, we offer our opinion and become involved with it. Now we have to solve someone else's problems.

I have a simple solution to have the quality of friends we expect. *Create a table of expectation for your friends as well.* What kind of principles and values your friends need to possess to have the chance to share time with you? No, you are not arrogant or cocky, you are selective. If you have goals and dreams, then find friends that have goals and dreams. The homeless hangs around the homeless. They have something in common. They understand each other well because they share the same philosophy.

ALPHA man must do the same. Find friends that share your philosophy. If you don't find them, learn to hang around solo. Fly solo, avoid bad company. Bad company drains your batteries. Don't make it a habit to depend on other people. Most of the time, they will disappoint you. They will not be there when they are needed. The true strength of an ALPHA leader is its willingness and ability to stand alone. So, be an ALPHA!

When we allow friends to invade our Drama-Free circle walls, we commence to carry some of their emotional infections. We might not be as stressed out as they might be, but we will be thinking about their problems and, that in itself, will cause a movement of emotions and feelings within us; feeling bad, sorry, pity for the person. We return to our home and bring those problems with us. We share them with our partner, family and friends. Without realizing it, gradually, we start to open up a door for this foreign drama to rest within our mind and heart.

Why allow and bring into our life and relationship negativity? It is better not to welcome it. No reason for us to invest our precious resources on foreign drama. Let others experience their own drama so, hopefully, they learn from it and grow as people. Why invest our resources talking about negative factors when we can be investing the same resources talking about our own future, objectives, projects, goals, and accomplishments? We should never allow ourselves to become a latrine for foreign drama. Don't give anyone the right to infect your Drama-Free Circle.

By the way, what is the quality of the friends you attract? Do these friends promote your growth? Are you attracting drug, alcohol, gambling friends? What you attract eventually you will become. Gradually the habits of other people will penetrate the barrier of your Drama-Free Circle. Everything starts with a beer with your friends, then a bar, and ends with you drinking often. You get the picture. Check out the friends you attract. If they don't meet your expectation, it is time to change friends. I know it is a cold truth! It is what it is. They have to follow their own way, so you can follow yours. Don't worry, they will find new friends, and so will you! And, when you find those new friends, you must decide who would you allow to influence and/or shape your opinions and your life. Even then, you have to be careful who penetrates your Drama-Free Circle.

Social Dogmas. Now, if you don't agree with the social dogmas transferred over by preachers, teachers, politicians etc., don't follow them. Simple. You don't have to carry in your subconscious a doctrine you disagree with. Inner personal debates cause stress and rob us from our concentration. Once you have figure out you position on social dogmas, stand by them. Don't justify your position or offer explanations to anyone other than yourself. You hold accountability to you, only! Follow what you like and agree with. It is your truth! It is you!

Here is a BIG ONE. Our parents play an essential role in ourselves throughout our lives. They always have something to say about how we ought to perform in life.

Many times they expect for us to become what they themselves were not able to become. Too many of parents have caused too much emotional damage on the life of their children to the point of pushing them away from them. They have ruined relationships for their children. Naturally, Mothers play an essential role and can easily influence their daughters. Men are more stubborn. A man should always be aware of this fact. Hold your partner and the mother accountable when Mom tries to penetrate your Drama-Free Circle. Don't know it and ignore it. The majority of parents mean well. They have knowledge on life. No one can take that away from them. If your parents are great examples to follow or even emulate, do it. Do you know parents you respect and admire? Especially, if they have the life style and relationship you want for yourself and your family? Listen up to them. Consider their opinion. But, don't be afraid to disagree with them on teachings you will not adopt. Sure, they are our parents. Show them you can think, too. We are capable of making our own decisions.

On the other hand, if your parents are not good examples to follow, don't follow them. Create, build, and chase your own legacy. Always be respectful to your parents, though. A matured, centered ALPHA offers understanding to everybody. Even if your parents lack greatly in knowledge to offer solid advice, we should offer our understanding and respect. When they become intrusive in our life and in our relationships, we don't allow them to penetrate our Drama-Free Circle. We need to stop them short. My friend, Ronny, married an oriental woman against his parents' will and acceptance; and so did she. They are the happiest couple on earth now. Politely, we listen to their advice, offer no rebuttal, then, we disregard it. Harsh! You can say that. But it is your life and you must live with the consequences of your acts. Parents want to participate in your happiness. But you have to decide how far and how they can participate.

Here I have another BOMB for you. Let's talk about women. Let's not be naïve about it. Let's be real. Usually, the nature of a person is their nature. People will promise adjustment to satisfy their own benefit and, then, will revert to their original state, to their nature, if you will. Let me share a fact with you that will make too many people angry. That's ok. I will not hide a truth, even if it makes other people uncomfortable.

Don't put up with a deceiving person. If during the process of getting to know each other she plays "good person" and then, suddenly, turns into an "ugly person" once she is with you, you have the act quickly. When that happens, you have to be able to identify that they hid their original nature from you. You must decide then if you will accept and put up with the new persona. If you put up with her unwanted behavior and attitudes, you will have opened the door for her to treat you as the submissive partner. She will become the ALPHA and you the BETA in the relationship. Whatever you decide is up to you. It is your personal decision. You will live with the consequences. What is important here is that you always have the right to set her in alignment with what you expect from her. Talk to her as mature adults no more than three times. No scolding, put down, or negativity. Screaming and fighting is for children. Talk as mature adults. First time you express your concern. Second time to remind her of your concern. Third time, let her go.

Do not make a habit to pardon her. I repeat: DO NOT MAKE IT A HABIT to become repetitive on your corrections to obtain an expectation. If you make it a habit, you would have acquired, unconsciously, BETA energy. Begging, complaining, and scolding your woman so she can behave the way you want is BETA energy. Stress, problems, tears, fights will start to show up in your relationship as a result of your complacency and acceptance of a behavior in misalignment with your expectations. You are the ALPHA male of your relationship. If your woman wants to defend her new state of mind, her nature, her new manners and habits, and you as an ALPHA do not stand up to her, then you will have to stand down to her. She will show you how an ALPHA should treat a BETA, and you will be that BETA.

If you make it a habit of over-suggesting corrective behaviors, you are toasted. Why? Because once you are the BETA in the relationship, she will start to seek out an ALPHA on the streets capable of guiding her and holding her accountable. Next thing you know, she is cheating on you and months later, she will walk away from the relationship. Why would she stay with someone she does not respect nor admires? As my female friend told once: "I only want that man to pay for my rent, my food, take care of the house, and to keep me entertained when the REAL guy is busy." Just be a strong ALPHA, because if you are not, she will be, and you will HATE it!! Holding on, strongly, to the ALPHA energy is the biggest challenge men confront nowadays.

We experience mental-paralysis when we need to defend our expectations. We feel as if we are bothering, inconveniencing, and disturbing the other person. We become passive. We don't want to confront anyone or anything to defend our ideas for fear of losing our partner. We conform. We think "well, I already have a partner with me. I already know how she is. I don't want to go to the struggle to find another woman; hell, it might be worse." We refuse to give our back to a bad deal. When you are not willing to walk away from a deal, no matter how good it is, you will have to submit to the person proposing the new deal. Again, you will hate it. You have no right to complain about what you allow to happen to you.

As an ALPHA, you should be willing to walk away from any deal, no matter how good it is, especially if it is in conflict with your expectations. I am talking about reasonable, humane, meaningful expectations. If you expect for your woman to do chores in her house and she does not do it, you don't physically abuse her and maker feel worthless. You sit down to talk to her as two mature adults and address her shortcomings. IF she consistently, continues to disregard your communication and the house is getting out of control, let her know. Tell her you will not accept that behavior. Once you allow one bad behavior, another behavior will pop out, and then another one, and so on until bad behaviors and attitudes become uncontrollable.

And this same advice applies to all men. If you know, or your woman tells you that you are not fulfilling your responsibilities as the ALPHA, sit down with her, listen to her, think carefully her suggestions, and resolve it at once. Just as you have high expectations for her, you should have high expectations for you as well. Don't ask from others to do what you are not willing to do yourself. Show her how it is done. Monkey see, monkey do! This is one of the greatest attitudes of ALPHAs. They are open to listening, talking things over, analyzing the information, and make the necessary corrections to follow the appropriate path. When they are wrong, they are fast to admit it and make the correction as well. ALPHAs value themselves highly. So, when they are not projecting their intended energy, they set their own selves straight. It is an innate ability they have developed with practice and time.

Pick one of these two scenarios. Would you be willing to undertake years of psychological and emotional suffering just to keep a person next to you that neither values you as a human being nor as a partner? Or, would you rather live solo without psychological and emotional paint?

Maintain control of you Drama-Free Circle. Everybody around you will try to penetrate your Circle. Defend your Circle by acting on your ALPHA male energy. You deserve peace and tranquility. Your life and your relationships deserve to be serene and enjoyable. Give others the opportunity to tackle their own problems and grow as people. Let them struggle and set them straight when erroneous; even if that means removing them from your life. Nobody will defend your Drama-Free Circle; only you!

19

KEEP THE FLAME BURNING AND GOING...

Gentleman, the courtship never ends. Courtship is the gasoline you need in your relationship for the car to keep up on running. The very moment you stop fueling the gasoline tank, stop courtship, the car wont' move, would settle, rust away, become old and monotonous, meaningless and useless, it would be just a car that you know you have, It does not mean much to you, it only occupies space in your house, sitting idle, waiting for it turns to hit the dump. The same is true with a relationship. We have to keep the flame going. We must keep pumping gas into it. We must keep the relationship vivid for as long as we are in it.

Let me share with you a powerful advice. NEVER allow, I say it again, NEVER allow your relationship to become monotonous, the same over and over and over again. Inject variety into your relationship. Every now and then change your hair style. Change the way you surprise, kiss, touch, play with, goof-around, look at, romance, and teas her. Change the way you dress. Alternate colognes, fragrances and jewelry. Switch around shopping stores. Experiment with new activities and distractions, freely. Visit different churches, bars, restaurants, museums, etc. etc. Create alternative distractions and entertainments. Be open-minded for it.

SPECIAL NOTE HERE: Be BOLD on bed. Lead her to express herself freely in the intimacy. Be audacious and fearless and show her it is okay to try new things out. Release your erotic and sexual urges with her and let her do the same, openly. She wants to hear your moaning, so let her moaning penetrate you mentally until every nerve within you feels her pleasure. She needs to see the wild part of you so she can turn into a tigress herself. She wants to hear your dirty words violating her lady-like etiquette. She wants to be dominated emotionally, mentally, and in multiple body positions. She must know you are also enjoying the moment, her body, and her pleasure. It is a man's responsibility to show her how to be experimental. She won't become experimental on her own; she needs a source of influence and approval: YOU. She needs to feel free, non-judged, and protected. She loves a gentleman on the streets and a wild-man in the intimacy. You, as the ALPHA male, must create and experience this world for her. She want to fulfill all her erotic fantasies with you. Be open and welcoming! Variety is what makes a relationship fun, because it makes everything different, fresh, and anew.

And that is what we need to do in our relationships. We, as ALPHA males, must be great leaders on bringing variety into our life. Women need to experience a different emotion, feeling, and journey constantly. Variety is what fuels the relationship to keep it fun and long-lasting. Variety is what keeps a woman madly in love with her man. Variety grooms creativity, thoughtfulness, excitement, and mysteriousness. Men must be consistent with variety. **VARIETY is THE KEY to building and maintaining enjoyable, life-long relationships.** That's what keeps the flame going and going! So bring variety into your life. If she does not find variety with you, she will look at finding it someplace else. Then, you will be done!

Below, there is a list of the most important factors I have discovered that keep the relationship burning for perpetuity. These are tools, actions every man must master and execute to build solid, enjoyable, long-lasting relationships.

1. **TIME**

   Time. The most important resource we have in this life: Time. When we are in a relationship, time is vital. Time plays a pivotal part within the relationship. The majority of the people have little conscience or have placed little value in their time. They invest too much time in causes or actions that impact their lives poorly. They invest most of their free time during weekdays watching too much television, sitcoms, soup operas, reality shows, news, and even idiotic shows displaying the life of other people. Many waste too many hours seating on the sofa admiring the ceiling while doing drugs. Friday is a drinking night until the body can bear no more alcohol or ran out of beer. Saturday is about recovering from Friday night and visiting friends to celebrate a particular occasion or special TV event. Sunday is a recovery day, again, football, soccer, movies, mall, and over sleeping. You get the point. Most of the time is about wasting time instead of creating a meaningful life, advancing our dreams. Most of us fall into this life-style pattern. We do these activities, individually. That is a problem.

An ALPHA male is responsible for raising the standard on the value of time. He needs to bring awareness to himself and his partner about the meaning and value of time. I am talking about quality time. See, investing quality time involves you doing what you like to do that is productive and effective. For instance if you both like going to the beach, dancing, bars, restaurants, malls, movies, traveling, etc. is quality time because you are with her, sharing time together. Quality time involves doing activities both of you like and enjoy, together. If you are watching a movie, are you watching the movie by yourself? Or, is she next to you on the sofa? Do you go with her to the gym or to walk around the block? Do you dedicate time for both of you for just goofing and joking around, children-like? Do you have dinner or lunch together?

It is important we understand how we are investing our time and whether we are getting the results we expect from the activities in which we invest our time. The majority of the time, women place little concern on time because they just want to be with you. Men are concerned about how they want to spend their time and, many times, they are not as concerned with whether or not the partner is happy doing the activity on hand. As an ALPHA male, you have to take into account she must also enjoy activities when she is with you. Every now and then both of you would run into activities one of you will not like. At that time, the dissatisfied person needs to understand those activities would occur rarely. The dissatisfying party should not mind compromising a little bit of time while the other person is happy. Problems arise when she is over investing time doing continuously an activity she does not like and enjoy. Now, if you make it a habit to just do what YOU want to do and do not acknowledge her likes and enjoyments, she will grow tired of it; just as you would as well. In the same way she compromises her time, you also have to compromise your time every now and then. Or, if she makes it a habit to take you to place you dislike, then say something about it. Stand up and clarify her perception of you doing that activity. So learn to compromise your likes and enjoyments to build up meaningful and purposeful moments.

Let me share the ATOMIC BOMB advice with you. It is that GREAT! Every week, at least once a week, date your partner. Once a week you take her to dinner, to the beach, to dance, to have a cup of coffee but, ONLY, your partner and you. Nobody else should be welcome to participate on this special date. No friends, no family, no children, no coworkers, no acquaintances, no body. This date belongs ONLY to both of you. ONLY BOTH OF YOU.

Make it a habit to perform this meaningful activity once a week. Some people use Fridays for their date out. You don't do it that way. It will become a monotonous activity. Don't make your date a predictable date. Otherwise, your dates will become a routine and routines lead to boredom; no excitement, no value, no flavor, no taste any more. You do not schedule a specific day to date your partner. Do it sporadically, any day of the week. Surprise her. Stay mysterious. Create anticipation. Keep her wondering about her next date with you.

Create variety. Invest time with her. Remember, 1. You don't tell her where you are taking her for the date. Let her wonder about it and allow her to enjoy the discovery experience. 2. You are her boyfriend and you want to listen to her 80 percent of the time so you keep on discovering her and everything else happening in her life, challenges and accomplishments she is experiencing. Use the remaining 20 percent of your time to ask questions about her conversation and share with her the new plans and objectives you are working on. 3. Take her to 2 or 3 different locations. Mall and restaurant. Dinner and dance. You know what I mean and always end your dates with the romantic activity last. Both of you need to give each other the gift of intimacy at the end of the date. You already penetrated her romantically. Now penetrate her physically. She will be expecting it.

Men are responsible to make sure that Dating and Courtship never ends. Time is extremely important. However, it is pivotal for you to be aware on how and where you are investing your time. Make sure you are delivering and receiving the satisfactions you both expect from each other at any given time and watch how no person will refuse to have a date with you. On the opposite, they are eager to have a date with you. People's ideas and feelings change with time. We, men, must keep up with these changes. These changes tell us how to conduct our life and relationship. A partner is important; so are the aging changes. Again, it is the man's responsibility to create the opportunity to date and romance his woman.

2. Appreciation

Give your partner appreciation. Give people honey and they will make you a favorite. They will smile when they see you because you make them feel good. The same is true for relationships and our partners. Treat them nicely. By giving our partner respect, value, and appreciation they will give us back the same; of course, assuming that the person you are with is a "good, conscientious person." This is the bottom line: offer encouragement. Praise accomplishments. Give value to every little detail or struggle your partner encounters. We do what give us satisfaction. If you notice she has a new hair-style, don't criticize, condemn, or complain about her new look. Instead, appreciate she is trying to improve her looks so she can feel good with herself and, at the same time, impress you. Don't focus on the little things that you don't like. Talk to her about the little things you do like and make a big deal out of them. Here is an example, my girlfriend gave me a ring with 5 stones around it. The stones were of different colors. I complained about the color of one stone I did not like. I criticized her about her choice and taste. I condemned her about the purchase. She kept quiet and just walked away from me. Two weeks later she arrived to our house with a new golden necklace. I asked her if she had purchased anything for me. She told me I should go myself to purchase what I like. This way, nobody gets hurt.

Another example. The night before Christmas, I invested over 5 hours of my time looking for the perfect gift for my girlfriend. Driving from mall to mall and walking from store to store. Tiring task! Finally, I decided to purchase a white-gold necklace with a nice diamond on it. I wrapped it up myself. She opened the gift during the family gift exchange session in the living room. She looked at it and said "Nice!" I felt good about her liking the necklace. It is not daily that a person receives a diamond! I kept track of the necklace's destiny. It broke my heart to see the necklace on the kitchen floor, behind the toilet, under the bed, under the kitchen sink, children playing with it, everywhere. My girlfriend did not appreciate nor value my time, thoughtfulness, struggles and hassles, my work or my money. She did not have to tell me verbally she did not like the gift. Her actions told me, loud and clear, she could care less about my gift. After that, she never saw another gift from me.

We are creatures of emotion. We like to receive praise and recognition for everything we do; especially women. They are fueled with emotions. Don't criticize, condemn or complain for the good things people do for you. Instead, be grateful and appreciative. People remember appreciation, but they remember criticism even more. In fact, criticism stays tattooed in a person's soul.

Criticism is *indelible*. You partner will recall how you make her feel every time she tries to express herself through a gift for you. Be tactful in your appreciation.

It is more meaningful and impactful to tell her how she makes you feel when she does a particular thing for you. Acknowledge the action, but make a big deal of the feeling by sharing with her the kind of emotions and sentiments you experience by receiving a gift and the value it brings to you. "Honey, the ring is pretty. But, you thinking about me makes me feel special." It is about how she or you make each other feel through the action. We live our lives from moment to moment, from feeling to feeling, and emotion to emotion.

3. Re-Assurance

Every now and then, we (especially women) have fears or doubts about ourselves and what we do. It is the responsibility of the man to reassure his woman. We need to reassure her that she is still pretty, attractive, provocative, seducing, interesting, fulfilling, etc. We also need to reassure her decisions. For instance, my friend purchased an "okay" dress for a special occasion. However, she was ecstatic about it because her boyfriend really loved it. She had her doubts about the dress at the beginning, according to herself. "My boyfriend reassured me that dress looked great on me," she said. So, she bought it. I asked her boyfriend if he really liked the dress. He told me he noticed his girlfriend liked the dress, but seemed confused about making a decision on it. "I reassured her that dress would look great on her. He said a couple of things he did not like about the dress. They were not that important to ruin a nice dress. Besides, once she had the dress on, I did not even remember those unimportant things." He focused on her and her happiness. The majority of the time, women already have the answer to their doubts; they just need someone they trust to provide reassurance on their decisions.

ADVISE: women find their answers by talking about the topic that is causing them a challenge, meanwhile, men find answers in solitude. So, when she wants to start a conversation with you on something causing her a challenge, simply ask her: "Honey, do you want me to listen to you, or do you want my opinion on it?" If she says to just listen to her, then, just listen to her. Have an attentive ear without offering your opinion. She is working things out, organizing her puzzle in her mind as she speaks with you. Get her talking by motivating her to think at a deeper level and by asking questions related to her topic. For example, "Tell me more about that." or "Say that again?" perhaps, "What you do mean by that?" also "What about it...?" or "So how would that work?" The point is to help her get in touch with her logic and reasoning. We help her by listening and asking well-thought out questions. You have to let her wrestle with the questions and answers.

Clarify that you are understanding her. Let her know you are paying attention by saying things like, "I am listening." "I see. Is that right?" "Okay, okay." "You mean..." "No kidding!" "Really!" "Very good!" You get the point. Your job is just listening to her. Do not offer your opinion.

If she needs your opinion, she will ask you for it. If she asks you for it, she is looking for reassurance on a decision she already worked out made and wants a second, trustable, opinion: yours. Here is an example:

Jenny, another girlfriend, showed up to work with a new hair-style. That style made her look younger and reborn. I told her so. She said she did not like it and did not feel comfortable with it. I told her it was normal to feel that way. She kept the same hair style for over 10 years and I told her so. I told her she was accustomed to seeing herself as she was and not as she is today. I told her that the old Jenny was fine, but the new Jenny grabbed everybody's attention. This Jenny looks different. She smiled and told me "Well, looking at it that way, I guess that's right." I reassured her: "I like it. I would not change anything about it." She thanked me. So, ALPHAs, find a way to make things right for the person. Once you make things right for the person, once you give the person honest honey, you get the "goodies." Don't offer dishonest opinions or reassurance. You would look fake and untrusting.

4. Help Her

A relationship is built by two people. The purpose of two people coming together is for them to increase their enjoyment, help each other evolve as human beings, and become more accomplished playing as a team. So, before moving together, you, as the man, must know if your partner wants to be a full-time, stay-at-home partner, or if she wants to work with no home chores responsibilities, or do what is most typical nowadays: work and home. It is essential for you to agree on the type of activity your partner will bring to the table.

If she wants to be a stay-home partner, then hold her accountable to the responsibilities she will be in charge of. If she wants to just work and provide, state with clarity who will maintain the house. Even if she wants to do both home and work, you must talk about responsibilities in the relationship and as a couple. Place the cards on the table from the very beginning, give no room for confusions. You need a way to know when either one of you is dropping the ball with responsibilities. Whichever way you choose is up to you. Nevertheless, let me share the following advice with you because the flame must keep burning regardless of your choosing.

We, as men, have the responsibility to be the main source of support for her to accomplish her goals. We have to listen to them. We already covered this topic in previous pages. Helping her does not mean we have to acquire her responsibilities at home or at work. She still has to pull her own wagon on these two areas. There is nothing wrong with you chopping the vegetable while she boils the water to prepare food. If she prepares food by herself, it is okay to volunteer to wash the dishes. It is permitted to bring the basket of dirty clothes to her so she can wash it. It is acceptable to help her with child care while she cleans the house or takes a shower. Baby-sitting the children while she attends school is helpful to her. If she needs to work over time every now and then, offer to prepare the dinner. You get the point. She needs to have that kind of support to evolve as a woman.

Our society will not take a step back. So, we as man, need to be able to redirect our relationships with women. Women need to have a solid partner capable of helping her and directing her on her journey to self-actualization. She wants somebody she knows she can count on and can hold her accountable for her actions and ideas. Men need to evolved with the idea that women must do more today than yesterday; be sensible but not submissive. Women want to also be good examples for her children to emulate. You need to be confident enough to grant her the necessary freedom for her to grow as a woman. As such, men need to remove some obstacles away for her without becoming one obstacle themselves.

You allowing her to evolve as a woman shows your trust and confidence on her. Now, there is a fine point here we must touch here. The moment she starts to take advantage of your generosity, good-will, kindness, trust and confidence, and you recognize it, and you don't say anything about it, that moment becomes a BIG problems. If we have to clean the house and baby-sit while she is drinking out and about with her friends and drinking is not approved, unless you already agree to that life style, which would be unacceptable. If she is watching a movie and there is no food on the table. It is intolerable to wear the same clothes for days because she does not feel like doing laundry. It is unsatisfactory to eat at restaurants in a daily basis just because she does not enjoy cooking in the house. You get the point. You accepting these type of behaviors mean that you are comfortable operating at BETA energy. If you are an ALPHA, you will hate this life style.

You are the man of the house. You are the driver of your relationship. She is counting on you. She will test you often to verify that you are still strong and solid as a partner. As an ALPHA, you have the responsibility to straighten the ship when the ship is trying to follow its own course. Correct the behaviors and attitudes you do not expect from your partner right away. Take actions to claim your position as an ALPHA in the relationship. Don't allow for your spouse or anyone to confuse your kindness for weaknesses or your trust for stupidity or your sincerity for naiveness. Lots of women in the world confuse the meaning of generosity, kindness, humility and trust. Be a good leader. Hold people accountable. Know when someone has passed the limits. You are helping her evolve into a professional and effective partner. You should never forget this fact. The moment a woman dishonors her responsibilities and diminishes you as a man, you have to set her straight or let her go.

5. **Participate and Be Present**

Get involved. Yeah, participate in the relationship and be present. Participate in activities that involve you and your partner. Participate with gusto! How many times has our partner asked us to accompany them to the store? How many times do we say, "You go ahead, honey, I'll just wait for you here at the house?" She ends up going to the store by herself, with her friends or family.

My 70 year old friend, Ronny, has been married for 55 years. He told me that we enter into relationships to create mutually benefiting circumstances. See, we enter into relationships to create memories together. The question is this: What type of memories are we creating when we are not present? When we do not participate in the memory creation process? Well, if we participate, we have something to talk about. If we don't, then we have nothing to talk about. We become boring. Here is the danger when we are not present and do not participate:

She goes out to the stores by herself. She will be surrounded by men and will run across a man willing to pay attention to her. He will look, contemplate, and complement her looks and presence. She will be flattered by such a man. She might not go along with a guy on the first approach, but eventually, one guy will break through her vail and she will become interested on him. She will accept that telephone number and, soon after, she is seeing that guy. Why? Because that guy took the time to be with her the time she was looking at dresses at the store. He made himself present! He told her how beautiful that dress look on her. She loved the compliment because she is not getting these compliments at her house. What is even more important is that the guy was PRESENT and participated on an activity important to her. He helped her make a decision. He reassured her decision on the dress. Where was her man? At the house! See, she wanted to get your reassurance before purchasing the dress. Since you were not there with her, she accepted the other guy's reassurance.

One of my friends told me he always hated to go shopping with his girlfriend. It bored him to walk behind her, pulling dresses out of shelves, modeling jewelry, testing new perfumes, etc. It was one of the most tedious and painful activities he dreaded to participate in. He desired to follow my advice. One evening he saw his girlfriend bored to death sitting around at the dining table. The perfect opportunity for him to test my advice. He approached her and told her to get ready to go out. She asked him where they were going. He responded that she would find out shortly.

So, out they went. He took her to her favorite clothing store. She complained with surprise. "You hate coming to this store with me. What has gotten into you?" she asked surprised. He held her hand and walked her into the store. Once inside the store, he selected a dress he liked and asked her to model it for him. She did. Then, another dress and another and another. He, himself, modeled for her some T-shirts she selected for him. They ended up buying something they both liked. Friday night, she decided to give herself a new hair look. Saturday, she proudly displayed her dress and her new hair style as she walked next to him on the mall. My friend told me that at that moment, he, finally, understood the power of being present and participation.

I asked him how he felt about this experience. He told me that "it was the most fun" he had had in many years. "It was something different. I don't know how or why I avoided this type of fun before. I felt like a boyfriend on a date!" He thanked me for the advice. I told him to thank himself for having the courage to face what makes him uncomfortable. He has made it a habit to participate in his relationship and be present with his woman. We follow norms and expectations imposed to us by friends and family; or movies. Sometimes we don't even know why. My challenge to you is this: challenge what makes you uncomfortable and see what happens?

Men need to participate, be present, and be involved with their women. Women need a partner in crime, a shopping friend, a lover on the side. Why not let it be you? What do you have to lose? Only her!!! Why not accept to go out with her when she invites you out? Go with her with gusto! Help her pick up the items she is looking for. If she wants to model anything for you, be present, let her. She just wants to make sure that whatever she buys is okay with you. So, when she walks next to you, she knows you are happy with it. Let's not fake tiredness. Or even if you are, pull some strength to participate and be present with your woman. When she seems bored, don't be afraid to volunteer to take her to her favorite places. Tell her "Get ready, we are going out." She will proceed with "Where?" You respond, "That's for me to know and for you to find out." Even here you must remain mysterious. That's unexpected for a man to do. An ordinary man. Not for you, because you are an ALPHA man.

6. Touch Her

We are creatures filled with sensations. Touching is the most powerful sensation we can give and receive from another person. Women NEED to be touched. They are emotional and sensitive. They are affectionate, tender, and sentimental. Physical contact is natural to them; it is their God-given nature. Physical contact is how they receive and transmit love, care, appreciation, humility, and emotions from and to others. So, let's touch them. Hold her hand. Hug her. If she is washing dishes, get behind her and kiss the back of her neck, bite her ear, rub slowly "little joe" against her buttocks, or just caress her skin just below her belly-bottom. Run your finger down from the top of her neck down to the end of the tailbone, gently. Playfully and gently pinch her nipples or just have a monster grab of her tits. Massage her entire body. Place your arm around her neck, her waist, while walking on the streets. Kiss her hand while she tries out the new ring. Caress her feet while she tries the new shoes. Play with her hair. Grab her hand while in the car. Lean her against your chest while standing up. Kiss her forehead when she expects a kiss on her lips. Touch her knee or leg when sitting across each other. You get the point. You have to be astute when and how you will give the gift of your touch. By touching her you send the hidden message that "she is still desirable."

Let me share with you a powerful secret. Your touching must be spontaneous. It has to be unexpected. The more sudden the physical touch, the more meaningful and more appreciation she assigns to your touching gesture. Too much touching is overwhelming. Be tactful rather than needy and romantic rather than a cloying partner.

Touching never ends. A women needs to be touched publically and privately, period. She needs to know she is valued and desired by her partner. She needs to feel sexy and sensual; feminine. Your touching gives her confirmation that she still turns you on!

7. **Watch her:**

Always admire her. When she walks on the street, as washes dishes, as she sleeps, when is grocery shopping with you, when she looks at you, any time you have the opportunity to appreciate her presence, watch her. When she showers take the time to inhale her fresh flowerily aroma. When she is dressing up look at her and tell her how she makes you feel when she gets naked in front of you: "Baby, I want to devour you completely every time I see you naked. You make me lose my civility." When she is not watching you, study carefully her eyes, nose, lips, hair, nail, eye brows, skin, hands, buttocks, breasts, toe nails, her feminine figure, and then, and tell her: "Gosh! You are my favorite drug. And I cannot get enough of you. You are beautiful." Tell her about your appreciation for her nice, supportive, loving, and romantic attitude towards you. The way she carries herself is sensual and provocative: "I appreciate you being so feminine. You make me feel like a wild Lion with an urge to attack you and make you mine." Every woman needs to know her partner pays attention to her: "Your happiness gives me happiness. I am glad you exist." She needs her man's affirmation that she is still provocative and desired; that she still can turn her man on! Women, just like men, love sensual, erotic, sex visual attention. The difference is that women keep it quiet and men want to brag about it. Women loved to be looked at, if they did not, they would not go through the daily beauty rituals and routines.

Now, if you don't want to look at her, some other person will do it for you. If you, as her partner, does not pay attention to her and make her feel desired, another person on the street will fit the gap you are not willing to fill in. The choice is yours. She is your partner. Don't expect from her what you are not willing to give. You expect for her to expose herself freely both inside and outside her body? She will do it, as long as you look at her correctly and lead her discretely. Looking at her is a perpetual habit. Don't take your eyes off her. She needs to know, ALWAYS, she is still attractive, seductive, and desired. This is how she feeds her self-esteem.

A MIRROR HAS TWO FACES

If you place yourself in front of the mirror, you see yourself. We see our reflection. We see us on the outside. We are the one that matters the most. Unfortunately, we only perceive one face: our reflection, the outer beauty. And, the same is true for almost 100 percent of all people, they see the same thing: themselves; their own reflection.

We forget we have two faces, 2 reflections. The one we see and the one we don't see; the outer beauty and the inner beauty. As an ALPHA male, you have to be able to see both reflections. This advice I received from a person that really cared about me. It would be unfair to keep this advice from you. So, I am going to share the specifics on how it happens. It worked and still is working wonders for me in my personal and social life.

I arrived to my friend, Tony's house, that Friday night. My physical energy and my self-esteem running low. I was disappointed with myself and with women, with my life itself; too many failures on all sides. I was unhappy about everything on my world. Tony gave me a cup of coffee and invited me to sit with him at his kitchen table. He asked me if I was open to hear an advice. I nodded my head up and down signaling him a thoughtful "Yes, I am." And he started:

Tony: "I have noticed for a while already that your batteries are running low. I can see the disappointment you tried to hide from the world. You think you are fooling everybody, don't you? The only one you are fooling here is yourself, Alfredo. Everybody senses something is happening in your life, but you deny it. I know something is happening in your life. I have known it, like I said, for a while. See, the easiest person to fool is yourself and you have been doing a pretty good job with it. Isn't that right?"

Me: "It is true.

Tony: "Alfredo, let me ask you a question: Are you happy with yourself? Do you like the person you have become up until today? Are you happy with your life as you live it today? Don't fool yourself anymore, just answer the questions to yourself with honesty and integrity."

Me: "No, I guess."

Tony: "Why?"

Me: "I don't know. It has being a while now that things are not going my way. Things seem to work out against me. As a result, I am feeling like a big failure."

Tony: "If there was a way to change your life and, as a result, your own self, would you actually take on the challenge and do it?"

Me: "Yes"

Tony: "Well, there is one; and I have it. A very successful man, in business and in life, shared it with me at a point in my life when I was feeling just like you one day. I am going to share it with you. He called it "The 2 Faces in the Mirror." This will be my gift to you. This is the only way I know how to help you. I will give you the information. You must decide whether to use it or dispose of it. The choice is yours, only yours."

Me: "I am ready, Tony. I am listening."

Tony: "Alfredo, a mirror has 2 faces. The one we see and the one that hides from us. Today, after our conversation, go home and stand in front of the mirror. Ask yourself these questions: Do I like what I see? Do I like the way I dress up? Then, take your clothes off. Do I like my body? Then, Look deep into your eyes and answer this question: Do I like my work? Has the way I think brought me what I expect in life? Go home now, and come back when you have an answer for those questions. Do yourself a favor, Alfredo, don't rush the answers. Take time to contemplate the questions carefully and sincerely."

I went back home. I took to heart Tony's advice and challenge. I was tire of being tired of being tired of being tired! I went back to Tony's house one week later with my answers written down.

Me: "Tony, I have studied the questions thoroughly. I can respond to your question with honesty and with great remorse."

Tony: "I am listening, Alfredo. Go right ahead."

Me: "I am not completely satisfied with the way I dress. I am disappointed with my body figure. I don't like my job, even though I make really good money. And the way I think has not brought me the results I expect to get in this life. I feel bad about all this. How did I allow this to happen to me? Maybe this is the reason why I am stressed out all the time and demotivated in life."

Tony: "See, Alfredo, when we invest time in taking care of the number one person in our life, us, we discover ourselves. We get to know ourselves more at a more profound level. We find our challenges and own answers. We find peace, release, understanding, and solutions. How can you expect to be happy with yourself, when everything you have going on in your life is working against you? You do not like the way you dress. You don't like your physical appearance. You dislike your job. Your thinking patterns are failing you. It only makes sense. You have been operating with the right formula to accomplish failure, sorrow, disappointment, low self-esteem, and stress. You have been applying this losing formula over the last years with the hope that it will get you different results. No way, Jose! And, as long as you continue to use the same losing formula in the next coming years, you will not reach a happy life. You will be the same person tomorrow as you were yesterday. Do you want to be happy? Then, you need to rethink your formula. You need to demand your own change. More of the same, brings more of the same. If you want your life to change, you need to welcome and commit to change. The choice is yours, only yours."

Me: "What do I do, Tony? I'm tired of feeling sorry for myself. I am tired of hiding my true persona. I know the problem now. How do correct it?"

Tony: "Alfredo, to be a happy person and to own a more enjoyable life, YOU MUST BE HAPPY WITH YOURSELF FIRST! Comfortable with whom you are! You cannot make other people happy, if you are not happy with your own self. The first step you take to start your personal change is by asking and answering your own tough questions. It should be your personal endeavor and responsibility to aim for your own happiness. Nobody can make you happy; only you. Only you know yourself really well. Only you know what motivates you and makes you happy. You are the only one who really understand your situations, struggles, and dreams. So, don't count on ANYONE, not even me, to suddenly build a life of happiness for you. You are going to have to do it yourself. Alone."

Me: "So how do I do it?"

Tony: "Go home, pull out a notebook and write down your answers and re-invent yourself! What kind of dress style makes me feel comfortable and satisfied? Visualize your new image or find the picture of a person walking on your favorite place and people looking at you. If you want to sculpture your body or just project a healthier you, then exercise and eat appropriately. Imagine or find the picture of a person that has the body you want to aim for. Find the job you like, become really good at it, and then the money follows. Are you getting this, Alfredo?"

Me: "It's making sense. I don't know why I did not think about this 10 years ago. But as long as I am alive, I can still do it, can't I?"

Tony: "Sure, you can! As long as you are honest to yourself. Almost nobody out there cares about you. Regardless, you should care about you. More essentially, you need to re-engineer your cognitive and emotional processes, the way you think and feel about things. You need to reprogram the computer in your heart and head! Redefine why you think and feel the way you do and make corrections as necessary. Establish clarity and purpose when adopting new ideas, emotions, feelings, and opinions. Select which dogmas you will pursue and understand **WHY** you are following those doctrines and teachings. Just as you re-invent your exterior image, you must re-construct the way you think. Exterior image is important, but it is more essential how you are built inside your heart and brain."

Me: "I understand."

Tony: "Identify and capture the new YOU. Once identified, start acting as the new you to form a habit. It takes 21 days for your body, mind, and heart to start getting used to the new YOU, the new habit. After 21 days, you will feel very comfortable carrying the image you have assigned to yourself. Don't think about the old you or the results you obtained as the old you. Instead, focus on the new you and the results you expect from the new you. Invest your thinking energy on the present to build the future; the past is the past. You do not have to tell me how you are progressing; I will be able to see it, just as you will see it too."

Me: "Thank you, Tony! I have invested plenty of time studying how to make other people better and this time, it will be ALL about ME!"

Tony: "Good! Have fun! And don't do anything you do not like and is congruent with the NEW YOU! Stand up for higher standards so you can attract other people who value higher standards as well. Alfredo, always remember that the mirror has 2 faces: the face we see and the face we don't. When things in life are not working out on your favor, take a look at the mirror, ask the questions, and start the process again."

IT WORKED! These first 21 days were physically and emotionally painfully. I had to change 25 years of monotonous habits. I saw my results 3 months later with a new physic, healthier skin and better image. My clothes looked a lot better on me now. I also found a Job I really enjoyed doing; it paid a little less than the previous, but my happiness makes up for the difference. I became more open to new ideas, concepts, dogmas, emotions, and people. This book came as a result of so much learning from so many great people; too many of them to enumerate here. I have everything I need in my life at this time. My life is filled with joyful rewards financially, romantically, and personally. It is too hard to explain it all here; you will understand me once you get there yourself.

You are the person responsible for your own happiness, just as you are the only one that will receive the consequences for your actions. My friends, if you want to be somebody that you have never been, you must do something that you have never done. I do not wish you good luck. I wish for you to develop integrity, intelligence, energy, discipline, determination, and the desire to be the person you are proud of. Make it fun! Enjoy your time in this life while it last. You deserve it!

21

SHARE AND TRANSFER THE SECRETS

Our time has come to depart. I appreciate your determination and discipline to finish this journey with me. I recommend for you to read this book no less seven times within a year. Then, read it once every year after finishing the 7 times as a refresher. I recommend you read it every December, just before the New Year starts and the old one reaches its end. Start fresh every year. Every business must evaluate its performance for the last year to determine if they had a healthy business or not. So, do us! We must assess our performance for the last year to ascertain WE are guiding our life in the direction we expect for it to go. If you like the way your life went the year before, then just refresh your mind by re-evaluating the factors working well for you. If you are not at the position you expected to be at the end of the year, then reposition your strategies; re-invent and re-engineer yourself, again. Re-building yourself is valid as long as YOU approve it and commit to it. So why not re-direct our life?

Why re-visit this journey so many times? Why read it yearly? Well, we are creatures of memories. We become comfortable and disregard or forget, what got us where we are. We start to conform and do not seek personal growth and wisdom any more. We tend to forget what is important to us. We have to remind ourselves that we exist and that we are valuable and important to our own selves first, then to others. What we repeat sticks. Repetition makes the maestro.

We have a machine. Our body and mind is the machine, we control both. We are the drivers of this machine. We drive and direct this machine. Are you going to let the machine drive itself into a hole and into a life of sorrow and hopelessness? Or, are you going hold on to it firmly and direct it the right direction? The choice is yours. It is your machine. You are the only one authorized to control it. Whatever you want to have, whether it's a wonderful life or a terrible life, the choice is there for you to make. You are sitting in the driver's seat. The wheel is in your hands for you to direct and control the machine.

You now possess the tools to build a joyous life and satisfying relationships. People should understand you and you should understand other people. The tools to reformulate your past and your future as you consider it necessary. Someone once gave me an advice. She said, "In this life we do not have we what we deserve, we have what we are willing to negotiate for." At the time, this adage did not make sense to me, it was meaningless, but now it does. Everyone deserves to have a happy and peaceful life, enjoyable relationships, a great family, a beautiful house with pool and open space, vacations to enchanting locations of the world, a nice car, and lots of money. Unfortunately, only a handful of people are willing to claim their stake on what they "deserve." They are happier seeing other people live the life they envision for themselves. They are not willing to put the sweat, energy, time, and sacrifice required to negotiate what they "deserve." They expect a miracle to happen to them. Basically, everything on this earth, Heavenly Father created for us and for our enjoyment; yet, only a hand-full of people will negotiate their God-given gifts; only a few people will enjoy those earthly pleasures. Again, it is a matter of choice and priority.

A matured, centered, ALPHA male must be willing to negotiate what he expects in life. ALPHA males always negotiate, they don't settle. They are always looking for the better of the best. They have dreams and objectives they chase after. When the circumstances are not on their side, they still find a way to get what they want by creating the circumstances. The life style you want is really yours. The consequences for the life you have set yourself to experience are also yours. Your life is yours and only yours!

My friends, here we end this journey. If you found this journey helpful to you, would you share and transfer it to others? Let's teach our children nuggets of wisdom early in the game, early in their life, what it means to be an ALPHA, a BETA, and a GAMA. Boys need to grow up to be effective ALPHA males. Girls need to grow up to be effective and proud BETAs or GAMAs. Why take a valuable secret to your grave? Let's be the example of the life we want to see. Let's help future generations become better people and create relationships with solid foundations, principals, and values. What spiritual, emotional, and intellectual legacy would you transfer to your future generations? Will they be better off when you check out of life? Or worse off? How would you like to be remembered? When we die, our bodies are buried in the ground. 5 years later, we get lucky if anyone of our relatives, let alone friends, visit our grave, gradually, we are permanently forgotten and we become something of the past. But, the concepts, ideas, teachings, doctrines, philosophies and the little sayings we teach our children, are timelessly remembered. They are shared and transferred from one generation the next. Just like my father used to say when he was alive: "What good is it to dream of something, if you are not willing to put the sweat behind it?" He also believed that "The way to better your world and the world of others, is by bettering yourself." My father told me that and I still tell that to my own children, and so it will go. So how will you be remembered? The choice is yours... only... yours. You are the leader of your life.

About the Author

Alfredo Mendoza, or Alfredo, as he prefers to be called, comes from a humbling background. Born in a below-poverty town of less than 1,500 residents. His family relocated to the city of Morelia, Michoacán, Mexico when he was 8 years old. Once at the city, Alfredo learned to make a living on the streets by selling chewing-gum to people, singing in public transportation buses and restaurants, polishing shoes, washing cars, and just about any money generating activity. As a typical child of the streets, or social parasite, as he was called, academically uneducated, he was destined to failure and poverty.

He became interested in personal development at the age of 9. His inner voice told him to keep on fighting for something better and he did. Upon his arrival to United States, he built a very successful janitorial services company. In spite of, his English language dominance being below the level of the American born/raised residents, he decided to attend Golden West College, where he earned his Associate in Arts Degree; although, it took him almost 6 years instead of 2 years to achieve it. Then, he attended The Minority Medical Education Program (MMEP) at Yale University. Eventually, he graduated from Chapman University with a Degree in Business Administration.

Upon graduation, he built a very successful organization within the financial services industry where he became top-10 ranking sales and trainer executive with an international financial services corporation. He has trained and coached thousands of people in finances, business, relationships, and in personal development. He is also an accomplished song writer, singer, and performer. He now oversees operations of a successful conglomerate family business.

About the REVIVE Institute:

Alfredo created the REVIVE Institute to help people, independently, or within a company, to experience a joyous life and operate more effectively as individuals using the REVIVE Strategy. Our vision is to teach people to teach themselves how to create and control a Drama-Free circle through the use of proven-principals and teachable concepts that yield everyday solutions. Our goal is to help people, who want to help themselves to find and increase personal value within themselves so they can function effectively as individuals, in relationships, and in business. We understand that when organizations have happy and mature individuals, these organizations possess valuable assets and a large competitive advantage.

The REVIVE institute works closely with small business owners, small and large companies, profit and non-profit, community organizations, schools, and cities seeking to help people to become effective contributors to their organization. The ultimate goal is to empower individuals to learn how to be self-reliant and team players when the organization requires it.

This empowering, REVIVE Strategy, is carried out through programs conducted at our local facility in Orange County, California for our international certified trainees and coaches. We also offer custom consulting services and personal coaching, customer on-site training, and client facilitated training as well as open enrollment, and workshops in many cities in North America.

REVIVE Institute offers a curriculum-based Coaching Training Program. Trainees are instructed to attentively utilize concepts and skills using interactive tools. Once coaches master our curriculum, they are set out to help and coach other individuals and companies. Every concept, lesson, and product is carefully selected to meet personal and business expectations. For more information on workshops and seminars closest to you or on how to enroll in our REVIVAL Coaching Program, please contact us at REVIVEinstitute@yahoo.com.

If interested about setting a special workshop, training or seminar for your organization, please email us REVIVEinstitute@yahoo.com. Tell us about your company and the reason or nature for the workshop or training. A 30-60 day notice is required for custom-workshops. Since we are booked considerably 6 months in advance, we will do our best to accommodate your workshop date based on a first come first serve basis. Thank you for your understanding.

REVIVE INSTITUTE:
P.O BOX 4368
Orange, CA 92865
Email: REVIVEinstitute@yahoo.com

MAN... Again is an imprint of
The REVIVE Institute, Orange, CA 92865
REVIVE Institute, Michoacán, Mexico

MAN... Again
Copyright © 2015

All rights reserved. No part of this book may be reproduced without written permission, except for brief quotations in books and critical reviews. For information, write REVIVE Institute, P.O BOX 4368, Orange, CA 92865,
Email: REVIVEinstitute@yahoo.com

The characters and events within this book are fictional, any resemblance to actual persons, places or events are purely coincidental.

First printing 2015

Printed in the United States of America

Illustrations by Alfredo Mendoza

ISBN-13: 978-0692515105 (REVIVE Institute)

ISBN-10: 0692515100

MY NOTES:

www.ingramcontent.com/pod-product-compliance
Lightning Source LLC
Chambersburg PA
CBHW070614160426
43194CB00009B/1268